Better Ethics NOW

How To

Avoid The Ethics Disaster You Never Saw Coming!

Second Edition

D1444788

What Others Are Saying About
"Better Ethics NOW"

"Christopher Bauer's book is practical and provides information that will help companies perform better. EVERY manager and executive can learn from reading Better Ethics NOW!*"*

Steve Odland, CEO,
Office Depot

"This book meets ethics challenges head on with simple solutions, keeping you from having to learn them in the school of hard knocks. It's a great handbook not just for business but for everyday life!"

Olen Parker, COO
American Design Drafting Association

"In Better Ethics NOW, *Christopher Bauer nails how to stop rationalizing your way through ethical challenges and take more responsibility for your choices. This is a book I think everyone should re-read once a year just to keep the message fresh!"*

Joe Rolwing, Director
Cumberland Emerging Technologies

"Christopher Bauer has given us some very straight talk about the single most important subject in business today – ethics. The great lesson from Christopher is that ethics aren't about 'the other guy.' Ethics are everyone's responsibility. If you want to build a business based on integrity, you should get Christopher Bauer's book for every employee."

Joe Calloway, Best-selling author of
Becoming A Category Of One, Indispensable,
and *Work Like You're Showing Off*

"Dr. Bauer's background, insights and experience make this book a true 'reality check' regarding how you and your company are dealing with ethics. It will give you guidelines, game-plans and goals to really focus your ethics program. Highly recommended!!!"

Frank Bucaro, Business Ethics Expert
and author of *Taking The High Road*

Better Ethics
NOW

How To

Avoid The Ethics Disaster
You Never Saw Coming!

Second Edition

Christopher Bauer, Ph.D.

Aab-Hill Business Books
Nashville, TN

This book presents a variety of ideas on how individuals, companies, associations, and other organizations can reduce their risk of ethics problems. It is written to educate and entertain its readers and is not intended to be a comprehensive guide to this subject. Additionally, not all ideas in this book have been tested empirically. This book is sold with the understanding that neither the author nor the publisher is engaged in rendering legal, accounting, or other professional advice. If you require such assistance, please seek advice from a competent professional. Neither the author nor publisher of this book shall have either responsibility or liability for any person or entity with respect to any loss or damage – whether caused or alleged to have been caused, whether directly or indirectly – by the information provided in this book. If these terms are not agreeable to you, you may return this book to the publisher for a full and immediate refund.

Cover and interior design by Ad Graphics – Tulsa, Oklahoma

Publisher's Cataloging-in-Publication

Bauer, Christopher, 1954-
    Better ethics now! : how to avoid the ethics disaster
you never saw coming / Christopher Bauer. -- 2nd ed.
    p. cm.
    Includes bibliographical references.
    LCCN 2007902607
    ISBN-13: 978-0-9765863-3-3 (hardbound)
    ISBN-10: 0-9765863-3-9 (hardbound)
    ISBN-13: 978-0-9765863-4-0 (softcover)
    ISBN-10: 0-9765863-4-7 (softcover)
    [etc.]

    1. Business ethics.   I. Title.

HF5387.B38 2007   174'.4
                  QBI07-600125

This book is also available in electronic form from the publisher and a variety of on-line resellers:
ISBN # 978-0-9765863-5-7

Quantity discounts of this book are available to your company,
educational institution, or professional association.
Please inquire by calling Aab-Hill at (615) 385-3523 or emailing to info@aab-hill.com.

Aab-Hill Business Books
Nashville, Tennessee
www.aab-hill.com

Contents

Acknowledgments

Many people helped shape this revised and expanded second edition of *Better Ethics NOW* and I am grateful to each of you.

First, I want to thank my clients, audiences, and readers for continuing to help me figure out which ideas are the real keepers. Without you, this book – as with its first edition – would have been much longer but in no way better. In addition, your comments have each been instrumental in guiding me as far as what best to revise and expand.

Of course there would be no second edition if the first had not come into being. I remain deeply indebted to the folks who were so very helpful to me in bringing the first edition to life. Frank Bucaro, Greg Maciolek, Kevin McNulty, and Joe Rolwing suffered through the very first, horrific draft of the first edition. Thanks to all of you, yet again, for your time, comments, and encouragement. Thanks also to the many people who later read more polished sections of the original manuscript and provided your thoughts. Shelva Suggs, Tony Hardister, Mary Kis, Olen Parker, Lois Forsmo, Jami McLeod, Michael Duncan, and Claire Hatch are among those who provided helpful feedback as the book progressed. I am extremely grateful to Joe Calloway and Phillip Van Hooser for their comments on the draft of this second edition.

Last but not least, my wonderful wife Carol has continued to listen to these ideas as the years and conceptual shifts have gone by. She has always been there to ask the hard questions and make the necessary comments. I am indebted – and will always be – to her honesty, directness, integrity, and love.

Better Ethics
NOW

Introduction to the
Second Edition

Can you recall the last time you read a newspaper or news magazine that did not contain a story about an ethics scandal or some sort? I certainly can't. Since publication of the first edition of *Better Ethics NOW*, the onslaught of ethics problems has continued, seemingly non-stop. Though hearty cheers are heard whenever some ethical wrong-doing gets righted, the fact remains that more and more ethics catastrophes are being discovered daily. Whether in business, government, the association world, or academia, we are all stunned by this seemingly ceaseless parade of transgressions, embarrassments, and horrors.

Despite everything we claim to have learned from being bombarded every day with new and awful disclosures of ethical wrongdoing, the estimates of the numbers and costs of ethics problems to businesses and the public are ever-growing. Add to that the media's on-going and often agonizing portrayal of the public's ever-diminishing trust in our corporations and institutions, and the state of ethics begins to truly look dismal.

Given all this, it is all the more startling to see how many organizations continue to keep their head in the sand when it comes to recognizing the need to develop effective ethics programs. They are either smugly certain that "it couldn't happen here," believe that a good compliance plan is all that is required, or simply assume that any possible problems will be caught before they get out of hand. Unfortunately, these beliefs all fall squarely into the category of hope as a strategy – a notoriously unsuccessful approach – and none support the development of programs for the prevention of ethics problems. Rather, they essentially set organizations up to wait and see, whether nervously or with apparently blissful ignorance, hoping that nothing too serious happens and, if it does, that the damage will not be too overwhelming.

Since the first edition of *Better Ethics NOW* was published, the continued onslaught of ethics problems has similarly continued to provide a field day for authors with books and articles on professional ethics appearing in ever-greater numbers. Each new author tries, in his or her own valiant and often compelling way, to help us understand this ever-expanding crises in corporate or professional ethics and offers suggestions about what we can do to manage it.

My problem with many of these books – as well as with untold numbers of articles appearing in magazines and journals across the globe – is that *I am not so sure we have much of a crisis in corporate or professional ethics on our hands.*

Really.

Now, I am not so naïve as to believe that nothing is wrong in corporate and professional ethics today. Clearly plenty is wrong. But I do not believe that corporate, association, or academic ethics are really the primary problem per se. Instead, despite the fact that we have some very real problems in each of those areas, I believe that the huge crisis we have been experiencing is in the taking of personal responsibility. And that is an extremely different thing.

Although this differentiation may well seem petty on the surface, it is far more than academic. It has significant implications for how we conceptualize ethics problems as well as how we work to help prevent them. Here is why; to adapt a well-known truism, companies, associations, and schools do not cause ethics problems, people and their personal problems and motivations do. Yet despite this, most ethics training focuses primarily or exclusively on teaching the rules and/or compliance mandates rather than providing tools for the identification of personal ethics risks and how to mitigate them.

Effective efforts to reduce ethics problems need to provide clear and easily applicable ideas on what to do about the individual and personal risks that everyone of us carries onto the job every day and that increase our risk for ethics problems. Knowing the rules is necessary but far from sufficient.

Ethics violators are usually fully aware of what constitutes appropriate behavior; yet they do not live or work by those behavioral expectations. Instead, their actions are driven by some combination of personal issues that only very rarely have anything to do with your business. They do not, for example, typically wake up in the morning and say, "Hey, this would be a great day to get my company into some big trouble!"; their goal in engaging in unethical or illegal activities is to take care of some type of personal gratification rather than the destruction of your organization.[1] On the other hand, they might well wake up and say, "I sure wish I could find an easier way to pay this mortgage. Surely it won't be such a big deal if I mess a bit with the books to bring in a little

---

[1] Besides, any sane ethics violator does not really want to hurt his or her company. Just like the parasite needs the host to survive, the unethical employee needs their company to survive in order to have a salary and whatever other benefits – financial, interpersonal, or otherwise, he or she derives from their employment. In fact, the overwhelming majority of ethics violators with whom I have discussed this never even considered the possibility that their actions would harm their companies in any significant way. Rather, they distorted their thinking in some manner to reassure themselves that their behavior was actually okay (i.e. "Sure this is helping me but it isn't hurting them.", for example). This is not to say there are not ethics violators with criminal mentalities out there since there obviously are. However, there are not nearly as many of them as we often assume.

more cash." Or, "I sure feel lonely. I hope I can find a way to get that new supervisee of mine to go out with me." Or, "I sure want my boss to like me. I know that he's bending some awfully big rules but I'd reaaaaaally hate to rock the boat. I like the guy, and besides, how am I going to get ahead if I make enemies?"

Each of the above scenarios can be the foundation for extremely serious ethics problems and yet none are actually about work; they simply get acted out at work. Each is actually about normal – even, perhaps, typical – needs and anxieties people bring onto the job rather than being about the job itself. Certainly none of these are about organizational governance. Rather, each represents an awkward incompatibility between a real or perceived personal need and the demands of appropriate behavior on the job. Acting on any of these inappropriate impulses represents a failure to develop adequate self-monitoring and self-control skills every bit as much or more than the failure of an organization to meet some type of standard of oversight. Of course, organizations are responsible for being vigilant to catch ethical and legal lapses as quickly as possible. However, my point is that those lapses are not *caused* by the organization.

This book will cover a variety of topics but will focus primarily on how personal values, needs, and aspirations – both those recognized by you and those not – can increase your risk for ethics problems and how to effectively recognize and manage those risks. Consequently, you will not find anything here on how to develop legal strategies to reduce your company's exposure in the courts, how to detect fraud, how to train compliance staff, how to recruit and train an ethics or compliance officer, or how to delegate authority and oversight to reduce the opportunities for legal and ethical transgressions. Each of those topics – and many more – are, of course, of vital importance in reducing your organization's exposure to ethics risk. However, each is beyond the scope and intentions of this book. Instead, this book is designed to help you learn what you can do to increase your abilities as an individual as well as the abilities of your organization, to really "walk the talk" of rock-solid, bulletproof, lapse-resistant ethics, starting right now. In fact, even when addressing organizational issues, the focus in this book will only rarely be on what others can do because better ethics will always start with you.

In addition, this book we will focus almost exclusively on concepts and tools you can start implementing immediately. Even though some will take both time and effort to see through to their maximum benefit, you can still begin to be put this book's ideas into practice today. I hope you will choose to do so.

So, if you are interested in doing your part to build and maintain your ethics as well as those of your organization – starting right now – this book is for you.

Just remember:

**The very best tool you will ever have
for improving your organization's ethics is you!**

Chapter One

The Real Costs of Ethics Violations

*"There's a hole in the moral ozone
and it's getting bigger."*

– Michael Josephson

For all the discussion about rampant ethics violations and their ever-mounting costs, what are ethics problems actually costing your business?

The easy answer is "A LOT"! Unfortunately, however, exact numbers are a bit of a moving target and largely depend on how narrowly or broadly you define ethics violations. To complicate matters, because new and different ethics problems of all shapes and sizes emerge every day, it is reasonable to assume that any quoted figures are probably both conservative and unreliable.

Here is a compelling figure, though: In the 1990s – but before Enron and all the other mega-scandals that began to emerge soon after – the Association of Certified Fraud Examiners provided what they labeled an extremely conservative estimate that United States companies were losing $400 billion annually due to white collar crime. *$400 billion*! And some experts have suggested that figure might represent as little as half the actual amount. Remember, too, that was the estimate before the discovery of the billions lost in the ethics debacles uncovered in the years during and subsequent to Enron, WorldCom, Tyco, Adelphia, etc. By 2002, the ACFE estimated that companies were losing a full six percent of gross revenues to white collar crime annually. In their 2006 study, the ACFE revised their estimate downwards to 5% of gross although, sadly, this may have had more to do with a change in their data collection methodology than to actual changes in the commission rates or costs of white collar crime.

In either case, though, even supposing that the ACFE's lowered figure is more accurate, that is still a truly staggering amount. Now, add to that the continuing, routine discovery of new ethics scandals of all shapes and sizes as mentioned above, and it strongly suggests that the already mind-numbing costs of ethics problems are still very much on the rise.

By any standard, the ACFE's estimates are dizzying. However, now consider that their study only reflects the direct costs of white collar crime and not other types of ethics problems. In other words, as colossal as these figures are, they represent only one piece of the ethics violation pie and do not calculate in a wide variety of other sometimes-enormous ethics-related costs. Among these many costs not calculated into their figures are:

- Legal fees and settlement costs related to discrimination and hostile workplace actions. It is not unusual for these to range from $250,000 to $750,000 with many now costing significantly more.

- The significant costs associated with contracts left unfulfilled due to a lack of appropriate or adequate oversight and the legal expenses that frequently accompany them. Add to that the huge legal fees and settlement costs associated with almost any type of professional incompetence and suddenly this category represents a huge potential financial sinkhole.

- The costs associated with internal inquiries into ethics problems and any required remedial actions.

- The expense of lost production time when employees are fired for ethics problems, recruitment costs to replace those employees, the costs of training newly hired replacement employees, etc.

Another missing figure is perhaps the most difficult to calculate but is quite possibly the biggest one of all. That is the enormity of losses due to lost business opportunity because of real or perceived ethics problems in your organization. Remember, potential customers', partners', affiliates', and supporters' perceptions of the credibility and integrity of your company or association can easily make or break their willingness to do business with you. We all want to do business with people and organizations on the up-and-up. Why should that be any different for someone thinking about doing business with your company or association?

In fact, do you actually know how much business you are losing simply because someone saw, heard, or felt something – however small it might seem to you – that led him or her to question the ethics, credibility, or reliability of your organization? The reality is that you may never know. Consequently, no matter how high the cost of your company's or association's ethics problems or potential ethics problems might seem to you to be, you have quite possibly only considered the tip of the proverbial iceberg. The frightening fact is that you could be losing business left and right due to ethics-related issues and never even know it. Further, should you ever find out, the damage will have already been done. It is the goal of this book to help you see what you can do – as an individual and starting immediately – to reduce your risk for ethics problems as well as the risk of your organization, no matter how unintentional or unconscious those risks might be.

How This Book Will Help

Most managers, executives, and auditors are used to scanning corporate governance documents, accounting reports, HR files, and board minutes to look for possible ethics weaknesses or lapses.

That is because we have come to assume that these documents are our essential window on ethics rights and wrongs. However, the most persistent ethics risks – the personal, social, financial, and emotional ones that we bring to work or the boardroom each day – tend to go either unnoticed or unaddressed exactly because they are personal and not organizational. In other words, we are stuck in a mindset where we look to compliance and oversight procedures to catch any and all problems rather than at ourselves to help prevent those problems in the first place. For the most part, this book will focus on exactly those kinds of personal risks that we all have and carry with us, however unwittingly, onto the job each and every day.

Because of our persistent reliance on oversight and compliance at a departmental, division, or organizational level, rather than prevention at a personal, individual level, many of the greatest ethics risks – which are simultaneously the risks over which we potentially have the greatest control – have a nasty way of creating problems that totally blindside us. We simply do not see them coming even though they look back at us in the mirror every single day. This book is primarily about how you can be more effective in monitoring and preventing those types of ethics risks while simultaneously helping to build the ethical resilience of your workgroup, department, division, or entire business.

In addition to helping you improve your self-monitoring for ethics risks, there will also be some discussion of how to help others develop a more effective focus on their own ethics. Last, some ideas will be provided on how your organization – as opposed to you as an individual – can build and maintain great ethics. The primary goal of this book, however, is to help you begin to develop skills as an individual for preventing ethics problems so that you and your company or association will not be doomed to the often-significant costs, embarrassments, and toils of cleaning up after them.

Why Is a Preventive Approach Important?

Why do I believe a preventive approach is so important? I will provide a variety of reasons throughout this book but here are two of the more important ones to start with:

1. "Don't worry. If there's a problem we'll find it."

> *"You can't put someone else*
> *in charge of your morals."*
> – Price Pritchett

It may be true that if wrongdoing occurs in your organization, someone will ultimately discover and deal with it. However, two very different problems exist with passively making this assumption.

First, most managers and executives do not discover ethics problems until they have either gone on for so long or become so significant that the damage is far beyond what it would have been if a more pro-active or preventive approach had been used. Also, the longer a problem persists and, therefore, the more institutionalized it becomes, the greater the risk that the inappropriate behavior will be thought of as acceptable. How often have we all heard about employees saying that they never blew the whistle on an ethics violation because, "I figured it was okay. After all, that's just the way we've always done it around here."?

Remember, your organization's culture and behavior can easily develop and crystallize around unethical practices just as easily as around ethical ones. Any number of inappropriate practices can become so much a part of your organization's fabric that no one even notices them anymore. In fact, like with so many other institutionalized problems, even if someone does notice the inappropriate behavior, they are much less likely to question it (i.e. "I guess this must be okay since no one else is speaking up about it." Or, simply, "Everyone else seems to think this is okay. I guess it must be fine.").

The other problem with passively assuming that someone will un-
cover any and all ethics problems is that – like with so many things
in life – prevention is always the ultimate weapon. Preventing ethics problems is simply cheaper and easier in the long run than
constantly having to clean up after them, even if you discover
them promptly.

I have been asked on a number of occasions how I can be sure that
the time and money spent on prevention will really be cheaper
than dealing with ethics problems after the fact. This has usually been posed by a manager or executive who wishes to take
an empirical, actuarial approach to ethics risk and they question
the appropriateness of investing in ethics and values training.
The blunt answer is that I cannot provide a dollar-for-dollar cost/
benefit analysis. However, nor can they offer an empirical foundation to refute the benefits of such an investment. As you read
this book, though, you will find a variety of reasons, extremely
compelling ones I believe, why even a modest investment in ethics and values training programs will have the potential to pay
off many, many times over for you. (And of course, on the other
side of the equation, who really wants to be known for advo-
cating that building and maintaining great ethics is a bad idea
because it may occasionally require a minor line item on your
training budget?)

2. "Other kinds of people cause ethics problems…
   not people like me."

> *"To err is human,*
> *to blame the next guy even more so."*
>
> – Anonymous

Perhaps in part due to the high profile nature of so many recent
ethics scandal perpetrators, many people seem to believe that significant ethics problems occur only at the top of big corporations

and that those problems are perpetrated solely by a rogue cadre of closeted corporate psychopaths. Consequently, they choose to presume that ethics problems are only issues in other companies and are caused only by people with whom they would never knowingly associate.

More and more, it fact, we seem to see potential ethics problems as something unrelated to ourselves and our organizations. This unfortunate type of thinking, however, is among the primary causes of unforeseen ethics catastrophes. We simply do not accept that anyone we know, let alone whom we like, could create such problems. We certainly do not accept that the person looking back at us in the mirror could be to blame!

In reality though, ethics problems can and do occur at all levels of all companies and associations, and the ghoulish, high profile offenders we read about so regularly are the extremely rare exception. These big cases simply make great press because of the perpetrators' flamboyance or celebrity and the frequently high dollar value of their transgressions. Because these high profile ethics scandals are the most visible ones – and because we feel that those people and their organizations are not like us – we can all-too-easily distance ourselves and our companies psychologically from the perceived risk of similar problems. Our rationale is, "That's just not the kind of person I am." Or, "That's not the kind of people we have working here." Or, "That's not the kind of company or association we are." Like it or not, none of those perceptions hold even a drop of water.

The fact is that otherwise perfectly normal people in perfectly normal companies, associations, and schools cause the overwhelming majority of ethics problems, both big and small. As jarring as it may feel, the reality is that simple. Ethics risks are not about "them" but, rather, about each one of us. Until you fully appreciate that, you will be doomed to miss your best opportunities to reduce your and your business' risk of ethics problems.

This book will help you discover the risks you bring to your organization's table every single day and things you can do to minimize those risks. Learning to do so is at the heart of a preventive approach, and prevention, in turn, is at the heart of how you and your organization can most effectively avoid the ethics disasters you never see coming.

The Basics

In order to effectively use this book, you must first understand a small number of key terms and concepts. Let's start by defining the word used more than any other in this book: Ethics.

What Are Ethics?

"Ethics are a code of values which guide our choices and actions and determine the purpose and course of our lives."

– Ayn Rand

Business and religious experts, philosophers, and countless others have discussed ethics and values for at least a few thousand years now. Consequently, you could easily read a lifetime's worth of philosophy and business theory only to have far more questions than answers about what ethics actually are. Despite that, as long as you are willing to forego an advanced degree in philosophy, you can create a perfectly functional definition of ethics without making it the least bit complicated. In fact, I will give you *three* simple definitions. Use whichever one(s) make the most sense to you since any or all will cover more than enough ground to serve you well.

Here goes…

1. Ethics are the moral guide we choose for our behavior. They are the sum of the ideas, experiences, information, and beliefs that guide us towards doing whatever we believe to be the next right thing.

2. Ethics are the rules we choose to follow even when no one is looking. In other words, ethics are not the rules: rather, ethics are what we chose to do with the rules.

3. Ethics are our internal moral compass.

The central theme in each of these definitions is that ethics are about your character and not about rules, regulations, or the law. Ethics can also be thought of as being the sum of your guiding values.

What Is a Guiding Value?

> *"Those who stand for nothing,*
> *fall for anything."*
> – Alex Hamilton

More elegant phrases probably exist for what I mean by "guiding values" but, be that as it may, the following is what I am referring to when I talk about them:

1. Guiding values are the values on which you base and judge your actions. In other words, if you look back at your behavior closely enough at the end of the day, your guiding values will be evident as the strongest thread connecting the rationale for your actions (i.e. "I tried to base everything I said and did on personal integrity." Or, "I tried to base everything I did today on assuring my customers of having the best possible experience with me and the company." Or, "Everything I did today was done to somehow make the world a better place" Or, "Everything I did today was intended to put extra money in my retirement fund and assure that I don't rock the corporate boat"). Your guiding values are those concepts so fundamental to what you believe to be important that they do not change regardless of what pressures you may encounter to change them or to refrain from putting them into practice.

2. Guiding values are the direct reflection of what you feel is most important about the choices you make (i.e. Do you believe that your choices must, most importantly, be made based on honesty? On clarity of thought? On allegiance to some type of political, religious, or spiritual belief system?, etc.).

One key to a preventive approach to ethics problems is being both acutely and persistently conscious of your guiding values. Why? Because, consciously or not, and regardless of whether or not you have accurately identified them, they are guiding your behavior all day, every day. If you are not conscious of what principles and values are guiding your choices, how can you possibly make any credible effort to effectively align your behavior with the values you claim to have?

When I conduct ethics workshops and seminars, I often ask the audience to start by jotting down their guiding values. Typically, each participant quickly scribbles down a list of several extremely virtuous-sounding ideals, most frequently crowned by something like, "Honesty above all else."

Of course, honesty above all else is a terrific value to hold. Unfortunately, in the real world, it is usually a lot of nonsense. In fact, our actual values are much more likely to be things like, "For goodness sake, don't rock the boat!" Or, "Never let your guard down with others," Or, "Do whatever it takes to avoid feeling anxious." Or, "Do nothing that will jeopardize my ability to look good to others." While these are much less virtuous-sounding, they are simultaneously entirely typical and entirely normal. We all want to look competent and strive to feel as comfortable as we possibly can. There is no shame in those pursuits as long as your behavior in trying to attain them is appropriate.

Even though the identification of these 'real-world' values may feel a little embarrassing at first, they are really not a problem in and of themselves. They simply reflect our humanness. Can they also be the cause ethics problems? Certainly, but not because they are intrinsically bad. Rather, it is because they represent values and risks we usually choose not to acknowledge to ourselves and so, in turn, we do not – in fact, cannot – monitor them; they are simply not in our range of awareness. By unfortunate extension, once we stop monitoring these risks, we open the door wider and wider for those less-than-virtuous-sounding values, however normal they may otherwise be, to do some serious damage.

Here is an example. No matter how much we rightly revere corporate whistle-blowers, "not wanting to rock the boat" by being a whistle-blower, in and of itself, never hurt any person or organization. However, if you do not recognize the fact that you would rather do anything in the world to avoid rocking the boat, then you will not ever be able to learn how to confront a variety of unethical behaviors in your organization (e.g. 'rocking the boat') in spite of your discomfort. The goal need not be comfort in rocking the boat. In fact, that is probably unrealistic. Rather, it is much more realistic for the goal to be for you to learn to do the right thing in spite of your discomfort. That goal, of course, cannot possibly be achieved without first becoming aware of what your personal discomforts are, even – or maybe especially – the ones that you would really rather not acknowledge, even to yourself.[2]

Ethics require making conscious decisions – every day – about the impact of your choices on the people you serve directly as well as the world at large.

---

[2] If analogy works better for you, think of it like this: A propensity for weight gain never made anyone fat. However, many overweight people choose to ignore their propensity for weight gain and eat considerably more than they should. It is not the propensity that causes the weight gain, it is ignoring the propensity and then not controlling or adapting your behavior accordingly.

The Role of Consciousness in Ethical Decision-Making

> *"In law a man is guilty when he violates the rights of others. In ethics he is guilty if he only thinks of doing so."*
>
> – Immanuel Kant

My beliefs regarding the role of consciousness in the making of ethical (or unethical) decisions seems to differ significantly from the accepted thinking. The above quote from Kant notwithstanding, here is the conventional thinking on ethics: Ethics are one hundred percent about behavior and have nothing to do with the thoughts behind your behavior.

The foundation for this well-accepted way of thinking is admittedly difficult to argue with and goes essentially like this: There are no laws against thinking about embarking on a spree of evil deeds. You can, for example, legally and ethically fantasize around the clock about strangling your boss or setting some new world record for the number of dollars successfully embezzled. Neither of these violates either the law or any tenet of any code of ethics because, thankfully, there are no laws against *thinking* anything. They only become legal and ethical violations when your thumb makes that first gleeful indentation on your boss' throat or when you pinch that first penny from the company coffers. This line of reasoning, of course, supports a compelling argument that ethics are exclusively about behavior and not about the thoughts behind the behavior. In fact, wouldn't it be a sad and terrifying world if thoughts *could* be illegal?

Here, however, is the central problem with that traditional and well-accepted line of reasoning. Habit governs most of our behavior, most of the time. It is not idle philosophizing to say that we are, indeed, creatures of habit. We do what we do because we behave reflexively, habitually, and automatically and do not change our habits without clear, conscious, and compelling reasons to do so. In fact, as most any cigarette smoker will tell you, we are such creatures of habit that some habits are incredibly tough to change even with clear, conscious, and compelling reasons to do so!

Among the many problems associated with acting on habit alone is that, essentially by definition, in such behavior we do not step back and examine our motives, guiding values, or options for making other choices. Yet without this type of very conscious self-examination, our behavior has far too many opportunities to drift – due to the habit-driven and unconscious nature of so many of our choices – across appropriate ethical boundaries, many times without our even being aware of it.

To state this more somewhat more directly; if we lack persistent, conscious attention to our behavior, we cannot possibly be self-monitoring effectively. And, without effective self-monitoring, we are significantly more prone to errors in both judgment and behavior. In fact, it is likely not an overstatement to say that a lack of self-monitoring is more or less tantamount to giving yourself permission to act in ways that are contrary to the values you would like for your actions to represent.

Remember how our actual guiding values are often not as virtuous as we might like to believe? Presumably, we all aspire to shift those values to ones about which we feel better. However, unless or until we are successful in doing so, we need to stay as conscious as possible of the risks our current crop of guiding values create for us. Perhaps needless to say, successfully changing your behavior to fully align with your stated values, once done, does not then excuse you from staying conscious of your thoughts, values, and behavioral choices in the future – that needs to be a lifelong process.

With apologies to Kant, none of this means that thoughts themselves can be unethical. Rather, I am simply trying to make the case that being persistently thoughtful, about not just what you do but why, is a critical foundation for reducing your risk for ethics problems.

What Constitutes an Ethics Violation?

"The right to swing my fist ends
where the other man's nose begins."
– Oliver Wendell Holmes, Jr.

Few ethics codes clearly or comprehensively define which specific behaviors are ethical and which are not. Consequently, defining what constitutes an ethics violation can be tougher than you might imagine. Further, because ethics and the law are not one and the same, a lack of clarity regarding what constitutes an ethics violation versus a legal violation is also a potential complication. In fact, a number of executives of large corporations have recently driven this problem home by, however lamely, attempting to defend against ethics charges simply by saying, "Gee, I always thought that was legal!"

However, without defining what constitutes an ethics violation in your organization as clearly and cleanly as possible, trying to clarify expected and accepted behaviors will be difficult. Simply put, you cannot reasonably enforce rules or values you cannot or have not actually articulated. Though that may sound obvious, it is amazing how many organizations cannot clearly articulate their values or behavioral expectations for their employees or board members.

Further, even if you have clarified and articulated your organization's values and behavioral expectations, if those values and behaviors are not then modeled by management and the board, it becomes extremely difficult to expect appropriate behavior from employees on the front line. In other words, if inappropriate behavior is modeled at the top, then inappropriate behavior is what you should expect from employees in return. This is yet another thought that might seem glaringly obvious and yet I will comfortably bet that you can easily name any number of businesses or associations where the behavior modeled by management or the board is jarringly at odds with the behavior said to be expected of the rest of the organization.[3]

So then, given all the above, what can you actually use as a reasonable, if general definition of an ethics violation? This is yet another topic about which untold numbers of books and articles have been written over not just decades but centuries, so there is no shortage of opinions. However, for the purposes of this book, I will suggest an extremely simple definition; namely that an ethics violation is caused by any behavior that:

1. Violates any ethics code under whose jurisdiction an individual is working and/or

2. Causes harm to an organization, its employees or members, its customers, or the community at large, through negligence or violation of the law, ethics code, or accepted standards of professional practice, in the absence of a conscious and thoroughly morally-based decision-making process.

In addition, there is an ethics violation whenever one's behavior willfully involves fraud or any other form of white collar crime, violates the civil rights of others in any form (age, gender, religious, or racial/ethnic biases, etc.), involves harassment of any type, or involves any form of willful behavior carried out specifically for the purpose of causing harm to others.

---

[3] Often making this worse is that managers and executives can have an uncanny way of suggesting that their behavior is actually acceptable *because* they are the management. In other words, there are explicitly different sets of ethical and behavioral expectations for different levels of employees. Lest it need to be said, such a disparity between what is acceptable behavior for managers or executives versus others is as bad an idea as they come. Among other things, it is antithetical to the development of a culture of ethics. Instead, it is a 'power-grab' that is completely demoralizing to employees, and – not just for that reason but for many more reasons as well – it truly represents an ethics disaster just waiting to happen.

A Preventive Maintenance Approach to Ethics

"You can pay me now –
or you can pay me later..."
– The Aamco Transmission Guy

I remember a now-ancient television commercial for a transmission company. The ad started with a transmission specialist standing in front of a good-looking car. As the bargain-basement price for their transmission inspection service flashed on the screen he said, "You can pay me now or...", (as the picture faded to a shot of him in front of the same car completely torn down into broken, twisted, filthy pieces around him), " you can pay me later." He was making a terrific case for preventive maintenance. I hope we would all agree that it is a sensible approach. After all, most problems, including those related to ethics, are more easily, cheaply, and effectively prevented than corrected.

So what is required to create an effective preventive maintenance approach to reducing your risk of ethics problems as well as the risk of those with whom you work? Whether at an individual or organizational level, the essential hallmarks of an effective plan are as follows:

1. A well-articulated and persistently applied statement of ethics and values (i.e. What do you stand for? What, to you or your organization, constitutes taking the high road? What are the behaviors you will use to bring those values to life? How will you constantly assess whether or not your actions align with your stated values?).

2. An effective process for assessing threats to your commitment to your ethics and values statements (e.g. Can you recognize red flags for potential ethics problems, whether personal or organizational, both effectively and efficiently?).

3. Clear, enforceable, and effective procedures for immediately dealing with red flags for ethics problems, once observed. Such procedures need to minimize both the risk of ethics lapses and the impact of any lapses that might occur despite your efforts at prevention.

4. Clarity that ethical behavior will be a cornerstone of your business practices and that you and your organization will persistently and explicitly notice, encourage, and reward such behavior while dealing swiftly, effectively, and appropriately with any transgressions.

Lest it need to be said, even a well-developed preventive approach will not keep all possible ethics problems from occurring. Prevention is a strategy – albeit a powerful one – and not a guarantee. However, the greater the amount of time and effort spent on prevention, the more fully and expertly you will be able to reduce the risk of ethics problems and intervene quickly and appropriately when they occur even in spite of your best efforts at prevention.

Despite the obvious advantages of a preventive approach, most organizations do not embrace such an approach. Instead, they say, "Don't worry. If there's a problem we'll find it" or "Unless we know precisely what it will save us, we are unwilling to even consider investing in prevention." In fact, at most, many companies and associations bring someone in to teach employees or members about the ethics code and the code of conduct, general legal requirements (and maybe EEOC, Sarbanes-Oxley and HIPAA if they are located in the U.S.), and perhaps run through a few ethics-related case studies. Is that information helpful? Absolutely! Is it sufficient? Not even close.

The type of training described above completely misses a couple of critically important components of truly effective programs for ethics risk reduction. The first thing missing is training to recognize the role of the personal values and working styles that each of us brings into the organizational mix every day and the ways in which they can set the scene for ethics problems of all types and magnitudes. The second missing component is training on how to assess the appropriateness of your behavior based on the degree to which it does or does not align with your personal values, the values claimed by your business, or both.

Today's typical approaches to ethics training largely or entirely focus on what the rules are and what horrible fate will presumably befall those who break them. There is no denying that employees need to have that information and, in fact, it is essential. However, to focus so exclusively on it misses critical aspects of what is required for employees to really understand ethics and ethics risk. It therefore inadvertently creates an unfortunate and significant barrier to truly effective ethics training because it only presents one portion of the necessary picture.

Maximally effective ethics and values training must show employees how to both recognize and mitigate what are perhaps the most persistent ethics risks they deal with all day, every day; namely, their unintended and often unconscious motivations for behavior that can cross ethical boundaries. They must learn how to evaluate their behavior as well as their impulses based on measures other than simply whether or not they conform to the rules. Additionally, truly effective ethics training teaches employees what to do when there *isn't* a rule for something. In other words, such training helps them understand as much about values as it does about the rules.

At the core of all of this is that really effective ethics training will help employees learn to judge whether or not their behavior is appropriately aligned with whatever values your organization has chosen to hold out as paramount. That is something they simply will not get if so much of their training is about learning the rules and not the values that those rules are intended to reinforce and protect.

Because current approaches to ethics training so rarely go beyond training on the rules to do any of the above things – let alone all of them – most can reasonably be judged to be both inadequate and penny-wise. In fact, many of these partial types of ethics training programs, however well intended they may be, can ultimately be extremely destructive because they create a false sense of security (i.e. "We did our required ethics training. I guess we must be safe from ethics problems now.").

Prevention will always be the ultimate weapon where potential ethics problems are concerned. Learn to practice 'preventive maintenance' with your personal ethics as well as those of your company or association!

Chapter Three

Ethics Codes: What They Do, Don't Do, and Should Do (And What You Need to Do in Either Case)

*"The most important thing in communication
is to hear what isn't being said."*

– Peter Drucker

Most of us have been trained to look first and foremost to our ethics codes for guidance on ethical decision-making. The code is, after all, the document charged with 'driving the train' of ethics in your department, division, company, or association.

So what do the ethics codes have to say about preventing ethics problems? Nothing much in most cases, as it turns out. But why not?

Ethics codes are frequently quirky documents. They are supposed to define for you what constitutes appropriate conduct, yet they usually prescribe very few specific behaviors. Or, in the alternative, they talk about behavior so exclusively that they do not discuss the values through which you are supposed to judge the ethical appropriateness of your behavior. Neither of these seem terribly useful for their intended purpose, frankly, because of what they do not cover.

In my experience, the overwhelming majority of ethics codes actually come in one of three impressively unhelpful varieties. The first is essentially a list of rules onto which someone has pasted the title "Ethics Code." The rules are obviously critically important and every company employee and association member needs to know them. But, as discussed earlier, an ethics code needs to be based on values and not just on rules; it ought to be able to help you decide what to do when there *isn't* a rule for something. So by all means, your organization needs to have a list of rules – just don't call it an ethics code!

The second type of ethics code I see more and more often these days is an even less helpful document. It is, typically, a forty to sixty page, single-spaced, dense, legalese risk management document – usually written by corporate counsel – and designed to protect your company or association from your behavior. Hardly handy in an ethical pinch, I'm afraid.

Another quirk of this category of ethics code is that they are often labeled as proprietary or confidential. I don't know about you, but I get immediately and intensely queasy imagining why a company would consider it inappropriate to let others know what their ethics are. Consider it worth investigating a bit if you are ever confronted with such a document and asked to adopt it. At the very least, find someone who can reliably translate the legalese into language you might actually be able to understand before signing on.

The third category of ethics codes represents by far the largest percentage of what is out there. Codes in this category come in all kinds of shapes, sizes, and language styles. However, once you strip away whatever language or format is used, they actually all provide pretty much the same few remarkably unhelpful admonitions. These codes each say, in so many words, some version of the following entirely obvious things:

- Do not lie. (Duh!)
- Do not cheat. (Duh!)
- Do not steal. (Duh!)

- Do not work outside your area(s) of professional competence. (Hopefully, Duh!)

- Do not enter into relationships or transactions that could impair your ability to deal with others in an objective and professional manner. (Hopefully, Duh!)

- Do not do engage in any behavior that would lead to a reduction in the perceived integrity, credibility, or desirability of your employer, association, or profession. (It seems to me that if you have been following the five prior mandates, you have probably already pretty much got this one in the bag...)

Most of the time, that is pretty much it. Anything very helpful in there? I would hardly think so. Again, it all seems pretty obvious, doesn't it?[4]

Mind you, there is nothing the least bit wrong with any of these admonitions. In fact, each is undeniably of great importance. However, if faced with some stomach-churningly difficult ethical dilemma, it is tough to imagine that any of these directives would tell you anything that you did not already know.

Many ethics codes are largely 'aspirational' in nature. That is, they talk primarily about what members of a business, profession, or

---

[4] It has long seemed to me these types of codes are written, in essence, like political campaign slogans in that they are extremely broadly-stated and positive sounding documents but are absent any specifics that will actually make them terribly useful. Have you ever, for example, known a politician who *didn't* run on a campaign of "truth, justice, and the patriotic way"? Of course not. It sounds great but we are all already supposed to have those values, anyhow. Despite sounding good, the slogan does not actually tell you anything about the specific behaviors in which you are or are not supposed to engage. This last category of ethics codes tends to include, at most, an extremely narrow range of actual behavioral prescriptions and what is prescribed is usually hardly startlingly helpful because they are essentially common sense admonitions just like the six mandates mentioned above.

association should "endeavor" to do when problems arise and no specific suggestions for behavior are provided. This can be quite helpful as long as there is clarity about the values one is to use as a guide in deciding what to do when confronted with an ethics problem where no other guidelines seem to exist. Unfortunately, however, such values are only rarely spelled out at all, let alone with the necessary clarity.

Sometimes, the lack of clear guidance in a code is merely a reflection that the writers recognized that in the course of working in the real world, some situations simply have no clear-cut right or wrong response. I would suggest, however, that those are exactly the situations – where there is no clear right or wrong response – in which we *most* need clear direction on which to rely in deciding what to do. Put another way, codes should be designed to give you helpful information about how to decide on a course of action when faced with an ethically complicated matter. They need not – in fact, cannot – presume to know the right response to every type of problem in every possible situation; the real world is obviously too complicated. And besides, if there is such an obviously always-proper response, it belongs in a code of conduct or list of rules because it is, in fact, presumably a rule at that point.

So should your organization's ethics code spell out more specific behavioral expectations? That really depends. As long as your code of conduct clearly spells out what an employee or member must and must not do, those expectations need not be written in the ethics code, ethics statement, or values statement. What is essential is that those behavioral expectations are spelled out *somewhere* and that you can verify that all employees at all levels have read, understood, and promised to embrace them.

In fact, consider the potential advantages of leaving the ethics code or ethics/values statement uncluttered with a lot of specific behavioral expectations. Doing so can allow employees to more easily and completely remember the content of those codes and statements. (Appendix E provides a model for this type of combined ethics and values statement.[5]) Obviously, though, you must still be sure that specific behavioral expectations and the rules are clearly spelled out somewhere and that they can be easily accessed and routinely reviewed by all employees.

To what else do your employees need to have easy access for review? They need to be able to easily find and understand the laws relevant to their profession and your business, your organization's standards of conduct, federal mandates regarding discriminatory and hostile workplace matters, legally mandated practices (i.e. Sarbanes-Oxley, HIPAA, and EEOC requirements, etc.), generally accepted accounting practices ("GAAP"), and the list goes on. Your business practices – and those of your employees or members – cannot possibly be reliably ethical until you and they know the required behavioral expectations from both within and outside your organization. You just have to remember that for you and your employees or members to work ethically – *really* ethically – will require much more than just blindly following the rules.

Why Isn't Following the Rules Enough?

"In civilized life, law floats in a sea of ethics."

– Earl Warren

Though we can easily forget it, following the rules alone does not make our actions ethical. How can that be?

---

[5] To my amazement, some companies balk at taking the time or expending the effort to create or fine-tune their ethics code or values statement. My guess, though, is that you would not be reading this book if you shared that reticence. However, you may certainly come up against others for whom the prospect of 'doing a better job of doing the right thing' is simply not a terribly compelling argument for taking on such a task. Should it be helpful to you for making your case, Appendix H provides a quick overview of a few other ways in which a great ethics code will bring value to your business.

Here is a pretty dark and extreme example, but one that does a good job of illustrating this point:

Consider the workers in the concentration camps in World War II. Were they following the rules? Absolutely. Was their behavior within the law? Virtually always. In fact, not only was their behavior legal, it was frequently commended by their superiors as an outstanding display of dedication to the national ideals. Horrible though it sounds to say it, many were great company men and women by the standards we normally use for such things!

But was their behavior the least bit ethical? Not even remotely. We certainly gave a resounding thumbs down at the Nuremburg trials to anyone who claimed their innocence due to having simply been following orders. So, was their behavior legal? It certainly seems to have been. Was it ethical, though? Not in any way, shape, or form.

Further, just as following the rules can be unethical, breaking the rules can have a moral or ethical foundation. Gandhi made his mark on the world by consciously, intentionally, persistently, and publicly breaking the law. He stated that the then-current laws of the land were unacceptable and that, in protest and as an intended agent of change, he was not only going to break the law but encourage others to do the same. Was he a pretty ethically informed guy? It would be tough to argue otherwise, don't you think?

Martin Luther King, Jr. is another example. Once again, here is someone who said that the existing laws were unacceptable and that the proper moral and ethical – not just political – stance was to break those laws and encourage others to actively join in civil disobedience against racial discrimination. Was his stance entirely based on ethics? Of course, even though his behavior was also consciously, intentionally, and persistently illegal.

Again, the point here is that following the rules, in and of itself, does not make your behavior ethical.

That said, however, the likelihood that you will ever encounter a situation in which you feel ethically compelled to break the law in the line of your professional duties is probably extraordinarily remote at most. In fact, you might consider writing some version of the following memo to yourself:

MEMO TO CONSCIENCE:
To: My Conscience
From: Me
Date: The rest of my life
Re: Claiming conscience as my guide when wanting to break the rules

Please be advised that, though I will require my actions to reflect my essential beliefs and values, I will also need to remember that claiming conscience as my guide is not, in itself, a license to break the rules.

Consequently, I will need to remember that breaking the rules, regardless of how ethically-based I believe my actions to be, will lead to exactly the same types of discipline, loss of my job, censure, potential loss of professional credibility, etc., that would be the case if I carried out those same actions with shamelessly criminal intent.

Let me please remember to have a problem-solving session or two in advance of any such illegal activities so as to assess my willingness to fully and personally accept the consequences for my presumably ethics-based choices. I promise not to use this admonition to avoid acting on my conscience. However, I will expect to use it to gauge my degree of certainty that I actually do feel compelled to break a known law or mandated professional practice to live by my conscience.

Thanks, in advance, for your understanding and support in this matter.

Respectfully,
Me

P.S. I hope that you will continue to offer your counsel and comfort if or when I sit in a dark jail cell somewhere for a few years and then work five simultaneous jobs to pay off my fines.

So, self-directed memos aside, what is the moral of the story here? Besides hopefully driving home that ethics and the law are not one and the same, it is to see that it is paramount that we all take complete and exclusive responsibility for our thoughts, feelings, and behavior. Sadly, though, many of us are prone to do anything *but* take full responsibility for our choices. We find it easier when we transgress to say things like, "They 'made' me do it." Or, "How could I have helped doing that?" Or, "It was my only possible choice."

Remember – and this goes well beyond ethics – that pretty much everything you do besides breathing and pumping blood is your choice. Now, will some choices be especially difficult to make? Sure. But never forget that the choice is still yours and yours alone. *Must* you tolerate other people's unethical or otherwise unacceptable behavior? *Must* you stay in a job you that you do not feel involves doing the right thing (or you simply do not like)? Of course not! Again, you may need to make some extremely difficult decisions about how best to respond to those situations. However, claiming the decision is someone else's is dishonest. The bottom line is that no one can *make* you do anything you do not choose to do. Claiming otherwise, in itself, moves you away from acting with full integrity simply because it moves you away for accepting complete responsibility for your actions. (And, of course, remember that inaction is, itself, a choice for which we must all also take responsibility.)

Of course, we do not live in a vacuum and so various situations and circumstances can make it very much easier to feel certain ways or make certain behavioral choices. After all, none of us is immune to external pressures and we are surrounded by a wide range of pressures around the clock. Unfortunately, when we start to feel any of that pressure, whether it is social, emotional, financial, or otherwise, we are much more likely to respond in a reactive manner and, in our reactivity, are much more likely to respond without carefully thinking our options through first.

In other words, it is our normal tendency to react to pressured situations more often out of impulse and habit than out of careful and reasoned response; that is an entirely normal response to pressure. Because of this tendency to act out of habit rather than out of well-considered response when under pressure, we will typically respond in certain predictable ways under those conditions. As a very simple example, it is a pretty safe bet that you would feel angry if someone poked you in the eye; it is simply a normal and predictable response. In fact, like so many of our reactions in the world, almost anyone could have accurately predicted that response and few would have questioned whether or not it was a 'normal' way to respond. It would also perhaps be equally predictable that it would be tough to find a way at that moment to excuse the eye-poker for his or her behavior, possibly even if it was accidental but certainly not if it was on purpose. However, the relevant question here is whether or not these reactions would have actually been your only options. And the possibly awkward answer is – absolutely not. It was a learned and impulse-driven response that, however predictable, could have gone any number of other ways

The point here is that no matter how tough it might be to persistently base our behavior on what we know to be the right thing, it can still be awfully tough to do when habit takes over. However, none of the social, emotional, or financial pressures the world can deal us relieves us from taking total responsibility for the inappropriate choices we make, no matter how normal or predictable those choices may seem to be.

The fact is that with insight and practice, you can respond to pretty much any type of pressure in any kind of circumstance in a variety of alternative ways. For example, if there is pressure to join into (or ignore) inappropriate activities on the job, the choice of whether to do so is yours no matter who is applying the pressure. The impulse to condone or engage in something inappropriate – whether to please others or to maintain your status – may be perfectly natural. However, like it or not, it is one hundred percent up to you to decide whether or not to give in to that impulse. Only you can make that or any other choice for yourself, no matter how difficult some of those choices will be.

When all is said and done, each of us needs to take full responsibility for the choices we make and the actions we take. Then we need to take complete responsibility for their impact. Period!

Chapter Four

Building Better Ethics Versus
Relying on Compliance Training

"Action indeed is the sole medium of expression for ethics."
— Jane Addams

Ethics are the thoughts, feelings, information, and experiences that inform our behavioral choices. They are, as has been said earlier, our moral compass. Compliance, on the other hand, relates to the structures, controls, and oversight that organizations put into place to assure legal and ethical behavior.

This is an important distinction for a variety of reasons. Of the greatest relevance here, though, is that the majority of "ethics training" and "ethics consultation" in the business world today actually focus on compliance rather than ethics. These commonly found training programs, for example, teach which behaviors are expected, and perhaps what will befall you if you break the rules. However, they typically have little or nothing to say about organizational values – and how to bring those values to life through your behavior – or the identification of personal values and working styles and their relationship to the risk for ethics problems. Consequently, they do not foster an understanding of the underlying motivations for ethics problems or how to mitigate their risk. They also usually provide little or no attention to techniques for the prevention of ethics problems beyond their admonitions to follow the rules and report those who transgress. They are, in other words, about compliance far more than about ethics and most are actually exclusively about compliance.

Further, too many of the few programs that actually do focus on ethics instead of compliance fall squarely into one or two categories of inadequately effective approaches. The first category merely teaches the contents of the often-not-terribly-informative ethics code and perhaps the code of conduct, all-the-while hoping that this knowledge, in itself, will be sufficient to reduce the risk of serious ethics lapses.

Though training on the ethics code is obviously an essential part of the foundation for developing and maintaining ethical behavior, this approach on its own is entirely insufficient. Frankly, the overwhelming majority of ethics violators know the ethics code inside out and hearing it one more time will probably not do much to shift their thinking. After all, their inappropriate behavior either comes from a lack of interest or knowledge about how to persistently and effectively monitor their risks for ethics problems or about how to control their motivations and impulses to make inappropriate choices. Simply going over the rules one more time strikes me as being unlikely to create the sudden inspiration for change.

The second typical type of ethics-based training focuses on case studies and talking through the options for responding to a few given situations or conflicts. Here too is an approach that, to a degree, is clearly of great benefit. It gives people the opportunity to flex their ethical thinking and practice solving tough ethical problems that may come their way. However, this approach, too, actually also falls into the 'necessary but not sufficient' category as far as training goes.

Why? Because no matter how beneficial the case study approach may be, we can only prepare for a portion of real-world ethical dilemmas via that method. What one learns from the case study approach has almost exclusively to do with problems where the individual recognizes that there is a dilemma at hand and, usually, what that dilemma is. After all, the case study problems could not be 'solved' if the problems are not identified. Unfortunately, however, outside of the classroom this situation does not happen nearly as often as most of us assume. Far too many ethics problems get out of hand precisely because potential or actual problems are not recognized for what they are.

Further, the case study approach more or less tacitly assumes that the individual faced with the dilemma has an undiluted motivation to resolve the problem in an ethical manner which is something else that, however unfortunately, is not always going to be the case in the real world. The case study approach, in other words, does not typically account for personal issues and motivation – or a lack of it – for ethical behavior.

Because the psychological underpinnings of ethics risk are so rarely addressed in ethics training, they can have an unusual degree of power to drive ethical lapses. After all, controlling something of which you are unaware is obviously a whole lot more difficult. Consequently, ethics risk reduction efforts with their sole focus on teaching the ethics code or through the primary use of case studies, usually provide an inadequate defense against these unconscious or unintentional types of ethics risks. That is simply because, again, both prevention and intervention are difficult with a problem you do not see you have or might have in the future.

Really walking the talk of great ethics requires that individuals and organizations become conscious of their particular, specific risk factors and not assume that simply knowing the right thing to do will resolve their risk for ethics problems. Of course, awareness of ethics risk factors will not help either unless individuals are clearly and strongly motivated to attend to them and companies are willing to build effective and efficient systems to train, promote, and encourage uniformly ethical decision-making. Consequently then, the development and promulgation of these last factors (e.g. awareness and motivation to use that awareness) need to be a central component in transitioning from a culture of intervention (e.g.

primarily a compliance orientation) to a culture of prevention (e.g. primarily an ethics orientation).

Does any of this mean that control, compliance, and oversight programs are somehow unnecessary or evil? Of course not! These programs are – and need to be – carefully designed and implemented in your organization to help assure both legal and ethical behavior. But why stop there?

Rethinking Your Compliance Plan

If you have one or more employees, it seems to me that you need to have a formal compliance plan. Though a discussion of how best to create one is well beyond the scope of this book, I would still like to suggest a way in which you might want to create a different type of compliance plan than is customary. And, if you already have a compliance plan, the same recommendation applies…

Why not consider broadening the focus of your compliance initiatives by adding programs specifically geared towards preventing ethics problems rather simply catching them sooner. And, if you are big enough to have an audit and compliance department, while you are at it, why not also broaden their role so that they become consultants regarding preventive measures rather than solely being after-the-fact detectives and interventionists? They have – or certainly *should* have – a huge amount of expertise regarding what it takes to prevent ethics problems. Why not put that great pool of knowledge to use in developing your risk reduction programs?

In fact, until it becomes a trend to reconsider audit and compliance departments' roles in this way, oversight and intervention may well remain the majority of business' primary method of defense against ethics problems. That is because it is the audit and compliance departments that are most frequently charged with developing procedures regarding ethics and a preventive approach is often entirely off their radar; such an approach has simply not traditionally been either their training or their mandate. Of course, the policies directing them to deal with ethics may come from elsewhere but the 'nuts and bolts' design and implementation or procedures often falls to whoever is charged with compliance, whether that is a single person or an entire department. So, unless they are encouraged to change their way of thinking by whoever hands them the mandate to create the procedures, prevention programs are unlikely to be on the organization's plate.

Thankfully, we have internal audit and compliance professionals, as well as external auditors, to help catch wrongdoing and the benefits of their work cannot be overstated. Wouldn't it be terrific, though, if your organization could use those same professionals' expertise to more effectively prevent legal and ethical problems in the first place? That will be much more difficult, however, until you give those experts the explicit mandate to expand their roles to develop more comprehensive risk reduction programs.[6]

The place to start any of this, however, is with the development of a commitment to create and nurture a culture that truly has to do with ethics as opposed to compliance alone.

---

[6] Some companies will argue that this is not needed because they already have an ethics officer or perhaps even an ethics department. But why not give those folks all the help they can get by teaming them up with your compliance experts? Besides, it remains rare for all but the largest corporations to have such an officer or department. Smaller schools may have them just like their larger academic brethren but, regardless of the school size, those individuals or committees are often kept more than busy enough shepherding Institutional Review Board ("IRB") issues and the like. So, they can also usually use some extra help in addition to receiving a broader mandate as far as their role in trying to develop a culture of ethics at their institution.

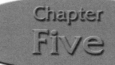
Where the Rubber
Meets the Road

*"A long habit of not thinking a thing wrong
gives it a superficial appearance of being right."*

– Thomas Paine

It seems to me that one of the most glaring reasons why unethical behavior is continuously found at all levels of the business food chain is that so many of us have simply stopped paying attention. In fact, some of us have become so accustomed to things being out of whack ethically that we now just numbly accept unacceptable behavior in ourselves or others. That, obviously, must stop for you if you want to make significant, positive changes in your organization's ethics. To admittedly state the obvious yet again, heads in the sand have never been a great foundation for positive change.

A Historical Perspective on Ethics in Business

*"The trouble with many plans is that they are based
on the way things are now. To be successful, your ... plan
must focus on what you want, not on what you have."*

– Nido Qubein

Let me briefly describe where most businesses started in regards to ethics, where some have moved to, and where I believe that every businessperson and every business needs to eventually get.

Here, however baldly, is the traditional view of the role of ethics in business:

Every
Technique
However
Insidious to
Compete
Successfully

A jaded sounding view? No doubt. But still, I will bet that you can easily recognize this approach in many businesses you know. Possibly, I dare say, you may recognize this as the approach *your* business currently takes.

In this model, all things revolve around the bottom line and little or nothing else much matters. If there is more money on the books at the end of the day than there was at the start of the day, life is good and things are fine. It does not really matter how you do it or who you run over, the goal is greater, hopefully immediately greater, profitability. In this model the old adage 'the bottom line is the bottom line' applies.

Let me be perfectly clear, I am not anti-success or anti-profit in any way, shape, or form. The more successful your business can be, the better. I just think that once the bottom line becomes a truly all-encompassing end in itself, you are significantly more willing to compromise on ethics and values in its service.

The task is to become clear on your principles and then – assuming that those principles are positive ones – build or rebuild your organization's culture and objectives to reflect and reinforce those principles from top to bottom. This process starts with you getting absolutely as clear as possible about what your values are as well as those of your organization. Then, again assuming that those values are positive ones, you need to be sure that your behavior and your organization's behavior are fully consistent with those values.

Lest it need to be said, clear values do not somehow interfere with success although I have occasionally heard some twisted arguments suggesting otherwise[7]. In fact, clear values can easily help build and sustain an ever-greater bottom line. After all, values are – or at least should be – something that unites all members of your organization in the service both of your organization and your customers. How could that possibly be bad for business?

By extension, in fact, a united organization – especially one with clear and powerfully stated ideals – will pretty much always function as a better team. And, wouldn't you agree that better teams typically do much better business? And still further, your values statement ought to explicitly encourage the kinds of behaviors that will build the most effective and efficient organization you ethically can. That, too, can pretty much only contribute to your success.

The Typical Corrective Approach to Ethics Concerns

In recent years, and usually in response to the increased scrutiny resulting from the glut of recent ethics scandals, many companies have left the previous model behind. In a great number of companies, I have seen the quick adoption of something like this:

Eradicate

Troublesome

Headaches through

Increased

Compliance &

Surveillance

---

[7] The usual argument, which I find disingenuous and, frankly, fairly bizarre, is that having an additional focus on anything besides profit will make it too difficult to simultaneously attend to each of your various priorities. Call me short-sighted, but I think that anyone finding it difficult to somehow attend to more than one priority at a time is awfully unlikely to have much success in the business world.

Is this a bad approach? Not necessarily and not entirely. Increased oversight helps to keep employees in line and all the new compliance office staff will help spot problems sooner, investigate them more thoroughly, and take employees to task if and as needed.

The idea that employees do more of whatever is observed or measured is well researched and inarguable. Consequently, increasing organizational oversight will certainly improve the consistency with which proper behavior is seen. (At least that will be true as long as the oversight is not so oppressive that employees want to leave or damage the organization out of frustration or spite!)

Depending on your business philosophy, increased oversight might feel like all the ethics program development you need. Many corporations certainly use this compliance-based approach as the cornerstone of their efforts to build a more bulletproof (or, perhaps, more litigation-proof) ethics program. As is, this model has serious drawbacks, however.

From my perspective, the critical problem with this model is that it inadvertently reinforces the idea that ethical practices need to be regulated from without rather than from within. In other words, this model – however unintentionally – enables people to be less committed to taking personal responsibility for their actions. Instead they can, in essence, go about their business as usual and simply presume that the compliance office will call should they have concerns. (I realize that this is a considerable overstatement. However, I believe that the underlying idea is a reality.)

Make no mistake – just as I am not anti-profit, I am also not anti-compliance. However, today's businesses, associations, and schools need to actively encourage employees at all levels to develop practices that incorporate fully conscious, ethically informed decisions and demand that those individuals take responsibility for the impact of their choices. Simply cleaning up after ethics messes, no matter how important that is, cannot and should not take the place of giving employees and members the tools needed to help prevent ethics problems in the first place.

Remember, everyone simply following orders is not the goal. In fact, a company of employees only doing what has always been done, with no questions asked, both opens the door to ethical problems and provides a terrific recipe for lousy business. Forget for a moment about the need for employees to question the ethics of potentially inappropriate practices; if your employees do nothing but what they have always done, without questioning why or generating alternatives, where will your innovations come from? Without that innovation, your company cannot even dream of staying competitive.

However, innovative thinking can only happen in direct proportion to the degree to which employees – with adequate training, information, and supervision – are empowered to make the suggestions and decisions they see best. Conversely, in the absence of such a climate, innovation is suppressed. Wouldn't you rather have company brimming with innovative ideas and employees committed to making your company all that it can be? In the same stroke, if employees are truly empowered and expected to use their judgment, they can also be simultaneously trained and encouraged to use those same powers of judgment to discern and carry out the types of behavior that are both appropriate (e.g. ethical) and which bring your organization's values to life.

A Better Model

So if the two previous models fall short, how do things need to be? Just like this:

*E*stablish
*T*houghtful
*H*onest
*I*nsightful
*C*ustomer-friendly
*S*ervices

This model may seem a bit general, fluffy or new age. However, it works extremely well. Why does it work so well and what does it take to implement? Here is a brief overview:

Thoughtfulness – Companies as a whole and employees as individuals need to be thoughtful about their values, their mission, their roles, and their personal impact on that mission and the world around them. More plainly put, you need to know what you stand for and why. After all, if you cannot buy into your mission, values, and role, chances are that you will not be able to perform well since you simply will not believe in your company, your job, or your mission enough to be enthusiastic about them. And without that enthusiasm, how can anyone work at, or even near, their actual potential? This, of course, also includes the enthusiasm required for working ethically but *none* of the above can occur until some amount of thoughtfulness has taken place.

It may well seem like this process of thoughtfulness has more to do with cornball personal or corporate success jargon than with ethics but, in fact, it has plenty to do with ethics. The reason is really pretty simple; until you are thoughtful about why you do what you do and how you and your company impact the world, how can you possibly know whether you are acting in accordance with the values you claim to have? Without sufficient consideration and introspection (e.g. thoughtfulness), you easily lose sight of both to what and to whom you feel that you ultimately need to answer. When that happens, you are suddenly making decisions in an ethical vacuum – you really have no way to judge whether or not your behavior actually aligns with your stated values.

Here's a critical detail regarding this process. I have yet to see anyone's job description mandating that a certain amount of time is to be spent on their being thoughtful about whether their actions are consonant with their values. At most, such a mandate may loosely show up now and then as a ten-minute agenda item at a rushed management retreat. Suffice it to say that those ten minutes are not going to be enough and that any other such thoughtfulness will not be an expected part of any job you will ever have.[8]

The reality is, in fact, that most jobs – including yours, I would guess – are so overly full with day-to-day work expectations that stepping back and being thoughtful about your behavior is the *last* thing you have time for! So, since no one else is probably going to make it a priority for you, make sure that you make it a priority for yourself. I cannot predict how long will be exactly the right amount for you. However, I will comfortably hazard a guess that *any* time you chose to put into it will be more than you do now and, similarly, that any amount of time you spend on this pursuit will be helpful.

Honesty – Employees, coworkers, and customers deserve to be told what is really going on and why. Without that, how can you expect them to really be a team with you? Obviously, some information is proprietary or premature to disclose. That is not a problem; it is simply part of business. But, aside from that, what could you possibly have to hide? The better information employees and customers have, the more effective they can be in making decisions and the better you can work together towards common goals.

From a business development standpoint, this is huge. For starters, you need your employees to be the very best team they can possibly be and that can only happen when they have consistently good information. Further, though, remember that if you have customers who really trust you, you are far more likely to retain them and there is not a lot in business more important than that! Do not blow either of these by letting it turn out that you have been feeding

---

[8] In fact, even if you are a corporate ethics officer, you are not likely to be required to do this. The closest you are likely to come is an expectation that you will be thoughtful about whether the company's actions and values align with one another and the law. An expectation that you will examine of your own ethics will not usually be an explicit part of the job description.

either your employees or your customers some line of dishonest garbage. Besides, the simple fact is that no one likes to be lied to. (Hopefully this is not a revelation for you...)

Perhaps you are among those who feel that your success is assured, regardless of your honesty, because your product is such a necessary commodity or maybe because you have a relative monopoly in your type of business or geographic area. First of all, never count on either of these carrying you forever. But either way, I promise that your teams will work better internally and that your customers will be far more loyal if they know that they can trust you.

If you believe that your department, division, or company runs better because the employees or public you serve do not know what is actually going on, that is as large a red flag for significant ethics problems as you are ever likely to find. Consider yourself warned.

Insightful – This goes hand-in-hand with thoughtfulness. If you really encourage individual as well as collective organizational self-evaluation, then more persistent thinking about your values and priorities will naturally result. It is reasonable to assume that, in turn, more time spent in thinking about your organization's values will lead to greater insight into when, where, and how those values can be brought to life through individuals' behavior and organizational initiatives. You may need to direct employees to think about that but, with even a little encouragement, it will happen. That process, in essence, is what I mean by being insightful.

In the way I am using it here, being insightful means paying attention to the impact of your actions on internal and external customers as well as the world around you. Maybe it seems obvious, but how can you really know how best to do your job or run your company if you have not taken time to understand what the impact of your job or product(s) actually are, why your job and organization actually exist, and how they impact others?

If you feel unsure about your answers to any of the above questions, there is no reasonable way for you to make fully ethically informed decisions as either an individual or as an organization; the lack of those answers deprives you of far too much critical information to do so.[9] After all, without that information you have placed yourself in an untenable information vacuum. Said more bluntly, without knowing the impact of what you do, you cannot possibly know whether what you have done is right or wrong by whatever standards you choose to use to make that judgment.

I am certainly not suggesting that an employee lacking the opportunity for thoughtfulness and insight will automatically be a bad employee or that, for some twisted reason, they should somehow be excused for willfully lying, hurting another employee, or stealing, etc. After all, you should not need an ethics code or code of conduct to know that those actions are unacceptable! However, without explicit encouragement to be both thoughtful and insightful, employees may be more prone to other more subtle kinds of ethical violations (i.e. unintended creation of a hostile work environment, unrecognized conflict of interest or restraint of trade violations, etc.), as well as reduced insight into the impact of potentially inappropriate behavioral choices. Such reduced insight, in and of itself, sets the scene for increased ethics troubles. After all, if you do not see the negative impact of a bad choice, you are much less likely to see that choice as a problem. And in turn, if a bad choice seems like no big deal, it is more difficult to make the case to yourself that you need to avoid making that choice.

Mind you, knowing that a poor choice will result in a negative consequence will not always be enough to keep a truly bad em-

---

[9] For that matter, how can you even possibly run a successful business without that very same information? My assumption is that it would be pretty much impossible unless dumb luck just happens to be enough to get you by for a while.

ployee from making that poor choice. However, training that bad employee in what types of behavior are expected – and the consequences for unacceptable behavior – has much more potential to help than to hurt! Not only that, but the risk of *good* employees making poor choices will be reduced once they are clear about the nature and extent of such a poor choice's risks to themselves and the company. Put another way, helping employees fully see the impact of their choices is likely to help them remember to do the right thing, whether out of fear or out of conscience.

As will be discussed in more detail in Chapter Nine (*"Just Say No To Just Saying No"*), to further maximize the power of this, you will need to help employees see the positive impact of good, pro-active choices and not just the negative consequences of poor choices. They need to have the power, authority, and encouragement to do good things as opposed to only having the expectation that they will avoid doing things deemed to be bad. Once they see the positive impact (e.g. how their own success if built) by going above and beyond merely what is expected by the rules, they will be positioned to become the superstar performers you would like them to be. This is hardly a novel idea, mind you, but is something that is somehow forgotten with remarkable regularity.

In addition to all of the above, it seems logical that employees who know their employer's plans, goals, values, and impact will be more likely to support the organization in any way they can because they can relate to the organization more deeply. After all, the more information you have about your organization, assuming that the information reflects values to which you can relate, the more of a sense of ownership you can comfortably take. And ownership is directly tied to improved performance, improved quality, and increased employee retention, each of which has tremendous value to you and your organization.

Furthermore, and above and beyond assuring employee insight, if ethical practices are one of the well-known cornerstones of your organization, and if you model and teach values and techniques that help assure ethical behaviors, then employees will be more prone to behave in an ethical manner. Why? The obvious answer is that it is because ethical behavior is what they constantly see modeled and encouraged. In addition, though, if they are helped to be insightful about how ethical behavior is actually a tool for their personal success, and not just for your company, that can be a powerful motivator in promoting and maintaining ethical behavior as well. Of course, no matter how helpful insight can be in building and maintaining ethical behavior, never underestimate the enormous power of good old-fashioned modeling, support, and a system of carefully targeted rewards.

Customer-friendly – Do you really have a clear idea of who your customers are? By that, I don't necessarily mean the average demographics of your end-user, even as critical as that information can be. Rather, have you thought about to whom you *really* answer? Is it your boss? Your boss' boss? Your personal values? The board of directors? Your religious or spiritual beliefs? The stockholders? Your political constituents? The customers of your end-users? Your local community?

Most of us, actually, have to answer to a combination of the above and their motives, wishes, and intentions are often anything but the same! In fact, how those various types of customers would like you to resolve any number of different types of problems is often wildly at odds with each other. So, to whom and for what are you going to choose to answer when those various customers' values or wishes clash? And at what risk to your job, integrity, or security are you willing to make that choice? Without having the clearest possible answer to these questions – however difficult any great clarity may be – you will be unable to fully assure a steady, values-driven (e.g. ethically based) course of action.

How you answer the tough questions can be quite different depending on to whom you ultimately choose to answer. Decide whom that is for you. The degree of your clarity on this will be directly related to the degree of your clarity regarding what to do when confronted with difficult ethical questions on the front lines.

Perhaps awkwardly, the more you choose to answer exclusively to your company, board, or shareholders (versus the community), the more pull towards ethical compromises you may feel. Why? Because the less you focus on your frontline customers, your community, and your company's impact on the world at large, the less likely you are to focus on anything but the bottom line. By extension, the more exclusively you focus on the bottom line, the more likely it is that you will feel pressured to make ethical compromises for the sake of that bottom line. Why? It is not because this somehow makes you a bad person. Rather it is because the bottom line will be the only issue on your radar and, very often, the radar of those people applying the pressure.

As mentioned previously, none of this is some roundabout covert stand against either profit or success. Rather, it is merely meant to reinforce the idea that the more exclusively you see profit as your company's sole focus, the more careful you must be to prevent being seduced away from your values and principles in the service of attaining that profit.

Regardless of whether or not your company chooses to be "socially responsible" by any of the various current definitions, remember that every organization has a financial and environmental impact – not just locally but globally in many cases. (In fact, if your company or association *doesn't* have some kind of impact, you are probably no longer in business!) Until you choose to pay attention to the nature and magnitude of that impact, you cannot possibly have adequate information to answer the tough questions about what to do when there are clashes between personal, community, and organizational values. Among a number of varied reasons, that is primarily because you will have no way to be able to understand your place in those conflicts. As a matter of fact, without looking at your personal and organizational impact, I do not know how you would even figure out that those clashes are occurring![10]

But What About Integrity?

You may have noticed that nowhere in my formulation have I mentioned integrity. Is that not important too? Not only is it important, but it is the *most* important thing where both ethics and business are concerned. So why is there no mention of it elsewhere?

Integrity has not been mentioned simply because it is not some activity you do or an initiative you create. Rather, it is a reflection of the degree to which you are willing to make every effort – day in and day out – to live by your stated values. It is both the cause and the ultimate effect of putting into practice the ideas I have just described as opposed to being an activity in itself.

Make no mistake, complete integrity is the prize on which you must most vigilantly keep your eyes. However, the path there is never a completely direct one since acting with integrity is a persistently multi-faceted endeavor; it is the sum of other parts rather than being one of the parts in itself. However, if you wanted to suggest a single goal or aspiration that is the one most likely to help you and your company to maximally reduce ethics risk while at the same time building the very most successful business, that would be integrity.

---

[10] Lest it need to be said, if you will not or cannot spot those conflicts, you are quite possibly on the fast track to getting blindsided by any number of potentially huge ethics problems. As has been discussed earlier, you cannot do much to mitigate the potential damage from a problem or potential problem that you do not choose to see.

From Theory to Practice

Putting the ideas in this chapter into practice will probably not require an investment of any significant new resources. Instead, at least to get started, it is more likely to simply require your willingness to think clearly and honestly about what your personal and organizational values are and what you would like them to be. Might you need to invest in some training or consultation in order to implement these ideas as fully and effectively as possible? Sure. But aren't you already spending time and money on making your company or association as effective and profitable as it can possibly be? Here is a chance to spend some of that time and training money on an initiative that will greatly benefit a wide variety of significant bases simultaneously. After all, even though the primary focus here is ethics and reducing your risk for costly ethics problems, everything being discussed will simultaneously help you create the foundation for highly effective values-driven initiatives that will drive better leadership, management, customer service, etc.

Said another way, stating that improved, solid ethics are a tool for success is not an overstatement. The ideas presented here will do more than reduce your risk of being blind-sided by ethics problems and their related costs. They will also help you build better teams, create clearer objectives, solidify your management philosophy, and focus more effectively on your customers' needs. Each of these falls squarely into the realm of pursuits that can improve your bottom line considerably. They just happen to be presented here in the context of ways to reduce your risk, and the risks of your company or association, for ethics disasters and the legion of problems that so frequently accompany them.

"Do all the good you can, by all the means you can, in all the ways you can, in all the places you can, at all the times you can, to all the people you can, as long as ever you can."

– John Wesley

Looking Into the
Mirror and Beyond

"The power of choosing good and evil
is within the reach of us all."

– Origen

As stated earlier, otherwise perfectly normal people in perfect-ly normal companies cause the majority of ethics problems, both big and small. It is that simple. No matter how much we might prefer to think otherwise, ethics risks are not about "them" but, rather, about each one of us.

Why Would Someone Like You and Me Violate the Ethics Code?

So why *do* seemingly nice, normal people cause so many ethics problems? Usually it is an attempt to deal with some completely non job-related matter through the job. It is amazing how small an unfulfilled desire for status, money, affection, attention, or se-curity is required for otherwise truly good people to compromise their values.

I have spent a great deal of time looking at the reasons people give for their ethical lapses. Although the reasons appear quite di-verse at first glance, once you strip away wording differences and the wide variety of excuses given, the underlying reasons all boil down to variations on the following few themes:

- "I just want to get ahead in life."
- "I just want more time for _____."
- "I just want to be liked/loved/respected/left alone by _____."
- "I just want to be a good breadwinner/employee/ colleague/partner."

Do any of these excuses sound heinous? Certainly not. In fact, most of them sound entirely upright if not conspicuously desirable. So how do they so easily bring us to 'the dark side'? Because each can also represent extremely strong psychological and emotional needs (i.e. for status, comfort, relationships, etc.) that, for whatever reasons, are not getting met outside of work. Work, then, offers what looks like a convenient – or sometimes the only – place to meet those needs. In fact, many times those needs, and our drive to try to fulfill them wherever and in whichever ways we can, are not even conscious unless we make it a priority to look for them. In the meantime, however, our attempts to meet those needs through the workplace can all too often be the starting point for behavior that crosses ethical boundaries.

Here is a quick but effective self-assessment you can use to scan for your personal potential areas of risk. Simply take a piece of paper and divide it into three columns. Label the left hand column "Guiding Values" and, under it, list the values you believe should govern your behavior. In addition, list those principles that you realize actually *do* govern your choices. As discussed previously, these will often be quite different from your ideals. But stay honest about what *really* drives your behavior and don't just list what you believe to be the socially appropriate or expected ideals. If you have not already thought about what those 'real life' values of yours are, this is a great time to do so.

Label the middle column "My Goals & Wishes." Under this heading, make a list of your personal and professional ambitions as well as the current aspects of your life you feel most deeply that you would like to maintain. This list might include certain personal or professional relationships, a desired income level, the pursuit of a certain hobby, activity, or relationship, something about your health, etc. Let the list reflect how your ideal life would look. This is for your information only so, as with the left hand column, you have no reason to be anything but honest.

The right hand column is the heart of this exercise. Label that column "Potential Conflicts." Now, scan the other two columns for items that have the potential to conflict with each other. In other words, do you see places where your 'real world' guiding values – and, perhaps, even the values you feel you *should* have – might get strained in pursuit of your ideal life? For example, if you have said that one of your guiding values is that you will always be honest with others, but one of your hopes is to maintain a comfortable business relationship with someone with whom you do not always feel you can be honest, identify it in the third column. If one of your values is that business decisions will always be based on ethics and not money, but one of your goals is to have a significantly larger personal bank account, might that create a potential conflict? If so – and it certainly might – put it in the third column.

Some items in the third column will probably be rather glaring as far as their need for monitoring while others will be much more subtle. Regardless, the goal is to be as thorough as you can in looking for potential conflicts. No matter how much or how little ends up in that right hand column, those entries can now become your "watch list" for places where your wishes and choices have a significantly higher potential, however unintentionally, to conflict with the mandates of ethical behavior. Attending to these areas, and updating this exercise periodically, should become one of the cornerstones of your self-monitoring.

Appendix C provides another type of self-monitoring tool and with a little research you can also find a variety of other ethics self-assessment tools on-line as well. As of this writing, I have found two to be particularly useful. The first is available at www. knowledgeleader.com and is a well-conceived, extensive list of ethics 'red flags' for both individuals and companies. Although written for use by auditors, I have found it to be a valuable tool for a wide range of job-types and industries. The second assessment is available at www.ethics.org (The Ethics Resource Center) and, though titled a "short-form" of their assessment, it is both a reasonably thorough and certainly effective tool for examining a variety of organizational ethics strengths and risks. Both of these are worth a close look and each can be easily applied to a wide range of types of organizations.

Even perfectly normal people with harmless intentions end up engaging in ethics violations of all shapes and sizes. Once you know the rules, persistent and effective self-monitoring is the single best defense against becoming one of them. In the meantime, simply being a 'good person' doesn't buy you an ounce of immunity.

Despite what most of us have chosen to believe, ethics violators are only rarely folks who are truly criminally minded. Instead, they are people so consumed by their needs and desires, however unconsciously, that they no longer monitor or control their behavior effectively. In fact, sometimes even entirely benign sounding desires can have a powerful negative effect on our thoughts, feelings, and behavior. Of course, the risk has little or nothing to do with the nature of the desires and everything to do with if and how you attempt to fulfill them.

Until you develop effective self-monitoring skills, you remain at risk for all-too-easily acting in inappropriate ways to get even presumably reasonable needs met. Not surprisingly I suppose, the first place to start looking for potential problems is in the mirror. Here's what that mirror might show you...

Recognizing Ethics Red Flags

We talk to ourselves all day long. No matter what the issue is, we keep a dialogue running in our heads throughout our waking hours. Consequently, these internal conversations are also just as present during any of our efforts to monitor and/or resolve ethical challenges.

So what kinds of things do you hear in your head when an ethics problem lurks somewhere nearby? The list of the most usual possibilities is actually quite short. Be concerned any time you hear yourself – or someone else – say any of the following:

"Whew! I just squeaked by on that one!"

Could this be entirely benign? Sure, maybe you just met a tight deadline, did a great job, and all is well. Terrific! Pat yourself on the back and move on. But when you hear yourself saying this, make sure it is really one of those benign reasons because "squeaking by" actually indicates trouble more often than not. It refers much more frequently to an unacceptable job that no one has noticed yet rather than a worthy job that was barely completed.

"I hope _____ doesn't find out about this."

Unless you are talking about planning someone's surprise party, you need to be especially careful when you hear this one. After all, how many people do you know who are so painfully modest that they lose sleep worrying that others will discover something *good* they did? I feel confident that those numbers are small. Something that someone else should not know about is probably something bad. The best possible explanation for this line is for some kind of communication problem (i.e. the work is fine but somehow appears not to be) and, of course, such a communication problem needs to be handled just as quickly and effectively as would any other important workplace problem. Plain and simple, any comment about hiding something essentially always indicates a problem, almost by definition. Pretty simply, the only questions worth following it up with are what exactly is the problem and what can be done to rectify it.

"_____ can always cover for me on this."

Once again, if you've done something that you need covered, chances are it was not good. Could it be something of no real consequence? Sure. Is that likely? Not really or why would you want to make your role in it disappear? And, if you find yourself thinking that it is just a small thing, remember that the stuff we consider small can often and easily end up having huge consequences for others and we might never even know it.

"Just this once…"

Perhaps because it sounds simultaneously so innocent, self-aware, and controlled, there is probably no more dangerous rationalization than this one. When you hear it, immediately remind whoever is saying it that an inappropriate action is no more appropriate if only done once. (And besides, if you really need to rationalize it before you have even done it, what are the chances of it being something you really ought to be getting ready to do?) Plus, once you have given yourself permission to do something wrong, it gets easier and easier to give yourself permission to do that same wrong thing again and again. Mind you, it is never too late to stop doing something that you ought not be doing. However, it is invariably easier to not cross the line in the first place.

"It's such a small thing; no one will really be affected by it anyhow."

Is a little white lie really ever really little or 'white'? Again, what is small for you may not be small for someone else. Are you having trouble being honest? Then work on your skills with directness and diplomacy.[11] Make no mistake, small ethics violations are still ethics violations. Are bigger one's worse? That depends who is asking and who is affected.

"Everyone else does it, for cryin' out loud!"

I cannot think of any possible benign reason for using this excuse. As has been said elsewhere and by a whole lot more people than me, we all need to take full responsibility for our behavior, no matter what others chose to do or why they choose to do it. Period.

Does hearing yourself – or anyone else – utter any of the above phrases absolutely mean that something awful has happened? Of course not. Thankfully, we are all innocent until proven guilty. However, any time that you find yourself saying or thinking one of these things – and any time you hear someone else make one of these comments – pay close attention to what is going on since each is a serious 'red flag' for ethics risks or lapses.

To say it again, *all* of us are susceptible to ethics problems. Simply saying, "I'm just not that kind of person," or "That doesn't happen in our company." is nothing more than sticking your head in the sand. So monitor your red flags every day!

What if You See a Red Flag?

If you have the slightest doubt about whether your actions, prospective actions, or those of someone else are ethical, start by considering whether they fit fully and comfortably within the values and commitments found in your personal, corporate, or as-

---

[11] Please remember, despite what most of us have had modeled for us our entire lives, diplomacy is not some kind of code word for lying! Being truly diplomatic means saying something that someone else probably doesn't want to hear but in a way that increases the likelihood that they will hear in the way in which you mean it and in the spirit in which you intend it. If anything, doing that properly requires scrupulous honesty rather than some kind of dodge of the actual truth.

sociation ethics and values statements. Following that, if you still have any doubt whatsoever, consult with someone who can help you determine the whether or not your concerns are warranted. And then, if you *still* experience even the smallest amount of uncertainty, consult some more.

We all need a well thought-out list of reliably available, credible peer and/or legal consultants with whom to review concerns about the ethics of our impulses and plans as well as the ethics of others. Not only will you be able to gather helpful information and counsel from these individuals, but utilizing them appropriately may also be helpful from a risk management standpoint. Case law tends to favor people whose actions followed careful consideration and timely consultation with others who have both objectivity and professional credibility in the appropriate field(s)[12].

The central goal of this type of consultation is to assess whether or not the behavior about which you are concerned is adequately in line with the accepted standard of professional practice. If it is not within the standard of practice, you are likely to have a very difficult time convincing others that it was an appropriate move. After all, if it is fully appropriate, why then is it not generally accepted as a standard of practice in your field?

Of course, there will always be new ways to do things – that is what innovation is all about – and those novel approaches may not yet be considered to be within the accepted scope or standard of practice

---

[12] Of course, having sought consultation is not a defense, in itself, for an ethics lapse. It does, however, show that you were thoughtful, honest, and appropriately concerned enough about your situation to seek credible advice. Investigators, ethics committees, and judges understandably tend to see that as a positive thing. Just be sure that your consultants are both objective and credible. Otherwise, seeking them out risks looking more like conspiracy than consultation! Also, both parties should document the consultation should there ever be a need to verify the nature, content and outcome of the interaction at a later date.

in your profession; probably, though, that is simply because they are still considered unique. Even in those cases, however, it should still be possible to determine whether or not they meet the essential standards of ethical practice (e.g. you are appropriately trained to perform or create whatever it is, there is a clear prospective benefit for your customer and it is not solely for your personal gain and at the risk of your customer, its impact will be appropriately monitored, etc.). If you have even the slightest doubt about meeting any of these standards, this is an area where speaking with a knowledgeable and objective consultant can often be extremely helpful.

Because so many ethics problems arise out of issues unrelated to work, your consultants list, however loosely defined here, needs to include non-work types as well. Doctors, religious/spiritual advisors, mental health and/or substance abuse specialists, financial advisors, etc., can all provide you with essential information and recommendations on issues you are facing outside of work that could negatively impact your ethics on the job. These consultants are not there to discuss business matters, of course, but matters pertaining to your physical, emotional, behavioral, and financial health. In other words, they will help you be sure that you take care of non-work problems outside of work so you can come to work with a clean slate. Remember, most ethics problems are due to non-work issues brought onto the job. If you take care of those non-work issues away from the office, your risk on the job will be directly proportionally reduced.

Are you a manager? A CEO, CFO or COO? A business owner? A board member? Developing programs to help employees reduce their problems in these non-job areas may well pay you back royally in reduced ethics problems, not to speak of the reduced lost time due to employee inefficiency, illness, and injury. (We will discuss this in more detail in Chapter 8.)

What else can you do if you see or hear a red flag and are not sure whether it represents a real problem? For starters, re-review the ethics code. It has probably not changed since last time you re-viewed it. However, sometimes a quick refresher will remind you of ideas or mandates that will help you resolve whatever issue is at hand.

Also, remember that even though ethics codes tend to change in-frequently – and minimally even then – interpretations of the code and case law continue to evolve. Find ways to stay abreast of those changes through professional journals, continuing education, peer discussions, or a combination. The more you know about these changes, the better prepared you will be when questions arise.

Now, will any of these techniques stop the problems caused by truly bad people in your organization? Probably not. That is really a matter of honing your hiring, training, and supervisory practices, combined with a hefty dose of good luck. Assuming, though, that your screening, hiring, and training programs are at least average – and, hopefully, they are much better than average – you should only have a very small number of truly 'bad apples' in your organi-zation's barrel. For everyone else, including you, the ideas in this chapter, as well as the rest of this book, will apply.

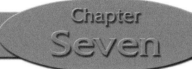

Chapter
Seven

What if You See an Ethics Problem?

"What we see depends mainly on what we look for."
– Sir John Lubbock

What if one of the red flags you notice turns out, as is often the case, to actually signal a real problem? After all, no matter how vigilant you are with both self-monitoring and the oversight of others, some ethics violations will occur.

Let's talk about what to do when you become aware of a problem, whether first hand or indirectly.

As a starting place, if the issue is internal, be sure to refer to your company's or association's policies and procedures. Depending on your organization, you may have highly detailed guidelines or regulations regarding what to do if you become aware of a problem. This will be particularly likely if you work in government or a company contracting with the government. Regardless of how detailed your regulations are, however, you need to know them from front to back. They govern – or, at least *should* govern – what you need to do in response to employee ethical and legal problems as well as the timeframe in which you need to carry out certain actions. If you do not already have these policies and procedures in place, make it a priority to develop them.

Developing these mandates and guidelines will help you to both operationalize and monitor essential internal compliance requirements. Once created, though, be sure that you follow those mandates and guidelines to the letter. Doing so will reduce your risk of legal problems due to not following the dictates of your own policies. It is important to remember that if ethics problems arise, showing that you followed your own policies and procedures in the investigative process, in addition to those mandated by state and federal law, can be extremely important. Not doing so can be construed as a serious ethics breach in itself, in addition to potentially being a legal violation. Also remember that your internal policies and procedures for ethics investigations must apply to every member of your organization and be enforced equally regardless of employee status in the company or community, stature in the employee's field, or job description. They must, of course, also be applied without regard to gender, race, religion, ethnicity, national origin, age, etc.

In addition to knowing and following your own internal policies and procedures as mentioned above, you must also be well aware of the relevant local and national legal mandates regarding ethics and accountability (e.g. EEOC, Sarbanes-Oxley, HIPAA, etc., or whichever apply in your country if you are outside the U.S.). Although reviewing and discussing these legal mandates is well beyond the scope of this book, you must know them thoroughly and adhere to them carefully. They define a wide range of legal boundaries in the workplace as well as a combination of guidelines and mandates for responding to concerns and complaints about their adherence. These guidelines and mandates are frequently quite specific and prescriptive. You and your managers must be well enough acquainted with them that you will be able to fully comply. Otherwise, a variety of penalties, and sometimes quite stiff ones, may well be awaiting you.

Ninety-Nine Percent Ethical Is Not Enough

I have been impressed and, I suppose, a bit *de*pressed with how frequently I encounter situations in which a company excuses or tolerates an employee's clearly unethical behavior because of all his or her other positive virtues. Perhaps these ethics violators are extremely knowledgeable in their field, have been a great mentor to others, have made notable contributions to the organization, wonderful financial contributions to civic funds, or contributed to any number of other terrific initiatives or activities. In many cases, these positive attributes are very real and their importance in no way exaggerated. None of those wonderful contributions, however, make it acceptable to take money from the company, make inappropriate social or sexual advances towards other employees, betray essential and/or legally protected confidences, or carry out any other unethical or illegal activities.

Not only do companies, schools, and associations sometimes excuse these individuals' unethical or illegal behaviors for the longest time but their behavior often takes an unduly long time to come to light in the first place. Because of the of the perpetrator's stature or status, his or her victims or colleagues who notice problems will frighteningly often say to themselves something like, "This person is so experienced and so well respected, I am obviously misjudging them." Or, "This person is my supervisor and must know what is right. I guess I must just be overly sensitive." Or, "This person has done so much good. I would never want to deprive the organization of this person's wisdom or him/her of their job." Their status often protects them from even being suspected or accused, let along brought to task.[13]

---

[13] If the issue is harassment or abuse of some kind and it is perpetrated by a supervisor, manager, or executive, their real – or sometimes simply perceived – power in the organization may be enough to keep subordinates from speaking up even in spite of recognizing some very real problem. In fact, almost any time there is such a real or perceived power differential between the perpetrator and the victim, it makes the harassment or abuse coercive by definition. That is, the harasser/abuser has or appears to have the power or authority to control the victim's work or life experience in some significant way and, therefore, the perpetrator is less likely to find resistance from the victim or be reported by them; the victim's fear of retribution will be too great. Individuals with this kind of coercive power can also hold significantly more sway when it comes to pressuring employees into joining or tolerating fraudulent schemes and other illegal behavior. However, that pressure does not excuse the employee for bowing to that pressure where duplicity in illegal behavior is involved.

To complicate matters further, just like other ethics violators, these folks – if they even stop to reflect on their actions – typically distort their thinking in an effort to justify their actions in some way. They might say, "This really doesn't hurt anyone anyhow." Or, "There is plenty to go around." Or, "I've put in my time, I'm entitled to this." Or, "I'm just trying to help make things look/feel/be better for this person/company/industry." Their denial and distortion, added to that of their colleagues, co-workers, and supervisees, often translates into a free pass to carry on with their inappropriate behavior for an unfathomable amount of time. Not all that infrequently, they are left to carry on their inappropriate behavior forever.

Here is the issue in a nutshell: Behaving ethically ninety-nine percent of the time is insufficient. A one percent ethics violation by an otherwise terrific person is still an ethics violation and needs to be addressed as if carried out by anyone else in your organization. Why? For starters, the damage to your company can be just as great, regardless of who causes the problem. But even more importantly, do you really want to be responsible for deciding that one person's ethics can somehow be more flexible than someone else's? At best that sets a lousy example but, in the same stroke, virtually assures you of having violated any number of legal and ethical mandates yourself. After all, doing nothing about a known problem – regardless of who the perpetrator is – passively supports the perpetrator's inappropriate or illegal behavior and creates personal culpability for you. In addition, enforcing rules differentially is, by definition, discriminatory.

When it comes to ethics, ninety-nine percent appropriate behavior is not enough. A one percent ethics violation is still an ethics violation and must be dealt with accordingly.

When to Respond to an Ethics Problem

Does the size or duration of an ethics violation affect whether or not you must respond to it personally and aggressively? As far as duration, the answer is easy; you must respond immediately in some manner. To do otherwise is to willfully, if passively, support the perpetration of the problem. Perhaps vexingly, the answer regarding the implications of the size of the problem to your response time is yes and no.

The following examples, though admittedly simple-minded, may be helpful illustrations of how difficult this question can be to answer a definitive manner:

1. No one would likely dispute that a senior executive embezzling $1,000 is more harmful to a company than a secretary taking home a $10 box of copier paper. Suppose, though, that ten secretaries each took home $10 boxes of copier paper. There has now been ten times the original amount lost – and ten times the number of perpetrators – even though the value is still only a tenth of what was taken by the executive. Would the ten-fold increase in losses require your response to be different than it was to the original lone thief's behavior? After all, a bigger share of company property would now have been lost.

    Now suppose, over time, each secretary took home *ten* boxes of copier paper. Would that then elevate the seriousness of their purloining of supplies to the same level as the senior executive's theft since the net loss would now be the same? And if you do consider the actions equal in impact, are all ten of those secretaries' actions now each as egregious as the actions of the senior manager's? Remember, their individual actions only netted them each $100 worth of paper and, in all likelihood, none of the damaging press generated by the executive's financial impropriety.

You might easily suggest that the appropriate response to each secretary's theft would be to let their immediate supervisors handle their case individually. After all, one secretary might be an otherwise model employee who simply messed up while another might have been a chronic problem employee with this being the last straw and, therefore, grounds for termination. This may be entirely reasonable thinking, but how will you respond when the latter employee sues and shows that your response to her theft was dramatically different than to the exact same action by someone in the next office? Also, will you be able to show, if asked, that the senior executive's actions were handled with the same degree of vigor as were the actions of the secretarial staff?

2. Suppose a manager "mildly" harassed a supervisee on one or two occasions. Surely that is less offensive to most people than a discovery that another manager has been seriously harassing multiple employees for many years. However, is the impact on the former perpetrator's victims necessarily any different than the impact on the latter's? Possibly not. And, from a more mercenary standpoint, is there any way to predict whether the legal and settlement costs will be less in the former case or that the public relations fallout will be any less? So many unknown factors exist that no one can really do more than guess.

The fact is that there are no obvious or absolute right answers to any of these questions. What *is* clear, though, is that you will almost always find yourself on an extremely slippery slope when trying to apportion or quantify the degree of "wrongness" of a given ethics problem. The issues are too complicated to reliably be able to do so. (And remember, the above examples are really quite simple in comparison to many of the matters that arise in the real world.)

Does this mean that every type or degree of transgression requires exactly the same style and intensity of intervention? Of course not. It does underscore, though, the benefits of having clear and comprehensive policies and procedures for handling all reasonably foreseeable ethics problems. You can then use those policies and procedures to deal equitably and consistently with issues involving everyone in your organization regardless of their rank, perceived importance, and the nature of their alleged ethics breach.

Just remember that even with a terrific set of policies and procedures, in the real world ethics dilemmas frequently do not have easy or perfect solutions. In fact, isn't the definition of a dilemma that there is a problem or cost associated with any of the available choices for resolving the issue at hand? Certainly, this is often the case with ethics issues. After all, if there were a rule covering it under any and all circumstances, you would presumably know exactly what to do. As has been said earlier, though, there isn't a rule for everything and part of the core of ethical behavior is learning what to do when there isn't a rule. Further, as the above examples hopefully illustrate, even when there *is* a rule for something, it can sometimes be an awkward challenge to know exactly how and when to fully enforce it.

What Else Can You Do?

If you become aware of an ethically questionable activity or a clear ethics violation that does not require a formal report or inquiry as per your policies or local/federal requirements, always start with an informal discussion with the individual about whose behavior you are concerned. Let him or her know what you have seen or heard and that you hope you have simply misunderstood or misinterpreted their actions. Ask for clarification and, if he or she has made a misstep, offer corrective information.

Most of us, frankly, would rather eat shards of glass than have such a discussion, especially with a friend or colleague. Be that is it may, though, such a conversation is unquestionably the most appropriate place to start. If you feel queasy about it, one way to fortify yourself might be to consider the Golden Rule. Think about it; if someone saw you doing something about which they had concerns, would you rather they asked you about it directly or started by going to your boss, the compliance office, the board, etc.? Though you may not revel in someone bringing a problem to your attention, I suspect you would greatly prefer that approach to the various alternatives.

Will such an informal discussion always go well? More often than you probably imagine and less often than you would probably want to hear. The bottom line, though, is that such a conversation is the proper place to start.

Sometimes the person you pull aside will be quite relieved because they felt uncertain or anxious about their actions. Sometimes they will be relieved simply because you did not take it to their superiors and gave them an opportunity to resolve the issue themselves. Maybe they had been working by strictly by habit and had truly not realized that their behavior was inappropriate. And of course, in more cases than we tend to consider, there are honest employees out there who are engaged in inappropriate behavior simply because they were trained incorrectly. Should any of these have been the reason for the inappropriate behavior, starting with an informal discussion will likely be both helpful and genuinely appreciated. If your informal intervention resolves the issue, you have fully and appropriately discharged your duty. If not, then you must takes further action.

By far the most important thing to remember is that doing nothing about a perceived problem is completely unacceptable. You must know how, when, and to whom you need to report a problem and then act accordingly. This is a classic case of, "If you're not part of the solution, then you're part of the problem."

What if the violation you see *is* egregious or continues after informal discussion? Then immediately report it to that person's supervisor(s), the ethics committee(s) and/or governmental oversight body with appropriate jurisdiction[14], your human resources department or compliance office (assuming the concern is internal), law enforcement, or some combination of the above. Here again, knowing your company's code of conduct, the relevant policies and procedures, and the basics of state and federal reporting mandates is critical. They will tell you to whom to report which types of problems and on what time line, as well as the manner in which to do so.

If you see something of concern but are not certain whether it is really a problem, this is one of those times discussed earlier where you need to consult, consult, consult! Perhaps that consultation will be with the ethics committee of your professional organization, a compliance officer, an attorney, or another colleague. Any or all of these might be helpful. However, for the sake of the person or organization about whom you are consulting, make every effort to keep their identity to yourself. After all, reputations can be ruined more easily than any of us would like to think and so efforts to assure privacy and confidentiality are imperative. This is all the more important since rumors and innuendo are often just as damaging as fact, and sometimes even more so.

Remember that regardless of what we like to think, presumably private conversations have a way of turning into tomorrow's news headlines. Consequently, the more you make an effort to protect

---

14 Remember that different individuals are responsible to different government departments, oversight entities, trade and professional associations, and licensing boards. The individual may or may not be responsible to the oversight bodies you assume. You may need to do some homework to assure that you are reporting to the proper person or body for that individual's ethics oversight. It does you no good to report problems to a person or oversight body that does not actually have jurisdiction.

the identity of the individual(s) about whom you are consulting, the better. Here again, think Golden Rule. You wouldn't want concerns about your practices discussed with people you know or with whom you do business. Restraint of trade issues can also be a concern, of course, and you need to be aware of what you can legally discuss with whom. If you don't know where those boundaries start and stop, educate yourself and the rest of your management team immediately. This is critical information and, of course, it affects far more than the do's and don'ts of ethics consultation. In the meantime, unless you know for certain that sharing information with someone about costs, fees, valuations, or contracts is okay, do not do it!

Does any of this mean that you actually *shouldn't* seek consultation regarding your concerns about others' ethics? Not at all. It simply means you need to make every reasonable effort to be discreet and protect the identity of the person(s) or organization(s) about whom you are consulting.

Even with due caution regarding the selection of a non-involved consultant (e.g. someone who will not recognize the case or the individuals involved), the best qualified person will sometimes be someone able to recognize the identity of the person(s) about whom you are seeking consultation. Should you find yourself in such a situation, it is usually best to choose the most qualified consultant even if they may be able to identify the person, corporation or association about whom you wish to consult. If, however, you are ever unsure whether such a consultation risks legal or ethical compromises, seek legal advice before proceeding.

Although you need to make any mandated ethics reports when a violation comes to your attention, you must be equally committed to avoiding capricious confrontations or reporting. Remember, aside from common courtesy, you must also keep from inadvertently making libelous or slanderous comments. In addition, you may well hold another person's or company's professional credibility in your hands, and messing with that is simply unfair. Even the creepiest people you know can still work in an entirely ethical manner. Similarly, many people's business practices are strange and maybe even repugnant to you. However, that does not mean they are necessarily unethical. Business can be conducted in many ways – even some really lousy ones – that are still legal and ethical. Reserve your confrontations and reports to oversight providers for the ones that are actually illegal and/or unethical.

To summarize, a legitimate and credible suspicion of unethical practices, even if unproven, requires intervention. Simply disliking someone or his or her way of doing business, however, is not a reason for a report or investigation! If action *is* required, do your best to start with an informal discussion if policy and the law permits. If a report is required, however, the follow-up can be via the proper person or oversight body, a formal or informal investigation (which one will usually depend on the nature of the problem), and/or through a variety of other direct interventions. Legal mandates, along with your policies and procedures should be able to guide you through the entire process with few, if any, questions or exceptions. Be sure you know – and that everyone in your organization knows – how questionable behavior is to be addressed.

If you see questionable behavior not requiring a formal ethics report, start with an informal discussion. If you find – with certainty – that this resolves the problem, you have discharged your duty. If, however, it does not resolve the issue, you *must* report it to the appropriate individual(s) or authorities.

Chapter Eight

What Else Can
Your Company Do?

"What we think, we become."

– Buddha

The primary focus so far has been on what you can do as an individual to solidify your ethics and those of your company or association. Let's shift the focus now to what your organization as a whole can do.

The Four Hallmarks of Effective Prevention

Earlier, I briefly mentioned four hallmarks of organizations that seem to do a better job than others of building and maintaining great ethics at all levels and over time. Let's talk now a bit more about how those four hallmarks can fit into the landscape of a business or association like yours.

1. Well-Articulated Ethics and Values Statements

Many companies and associations completely lack formal ethics or values statements while others' are so unclear as to be completely useless for guiding decisions. For example, "We do good things for people," or, "We value service," may be great mottos for public relations purposes but, in order for your employees to make use of them, they need both more specificity and context.

Articulate as clearly as possible what good things you plan to do or define what "service" actually means and, at least generally, through which means you expect employees to demonstrate those values. For example, will it be through the way staff and customers are treated? If so, how? Will it be through the embodiment or enforcement of certain values? If so, what are those values? Might it be through the kinds of products sold? Through philanthropy? Through community relationships or community service?

Your ethics and values statements do not need to be either long or complicated. In fact, shorter and simpler are usually better because that way they can be more easily memorized. Regardless of their length, however, they need to be clear, "do-able" and honest. If the details you wish employees to be aware of are too extensive to allow you to be concise, that's fine; not everything needs to be included in the body of those statements. If you prefer, many or maybe even most of those details can go into a code of conduct, any variety of HR documents, employee pamphlets received by everyone, an easily accessible intranet website, etc. After all, your ethics and values statements' clarity and ease of digestion are essential. If not everything fits neatly into those documents, that's fine; just be sure to write the details down *somewhere* and then be sure you regularly reference and expose all employees to them.

To see a model for integrating your ethics and values statements into a single, easily recalled and easily applied document, see Appendix E.

2. Effective Processes for Assessing Threats to Ethics and Compliance

Organizations frequently pay too little attention to this. Because after-the-fact audit and compliance structures typically take the place of effective prevention programs, most or all of companies' and associations' ethics improvement eggs are in the audit and compliance baskets. Any other ethics-improvement efforts either fall into the category of disciplinary action for ethics lapses or the kinds of inadequate training programs discussed earlier (i.e. simply going over the ethics code, the corporate/association code of conduct, the laws relating to any given group of employees, and maybe using a few case studies, etc.).

Without a focus on the role of personal issues and motivations in the development of ethics problems or a discussion of prevention tools, many employees may genuinely try to work ethically but have one hand tied behind their back. Even though their intentions may be fine, they simply have inadequate information and training to either build and maintain their ethics to their maximum potential or effectively assess the ethics of those with whom they work. Each of these is a threat to your organization's ethics and both are likely to fly under your radar until you make it a point pay explicit and persistent attention to them.

If your company or association really wants to prevent ethics problems rather than clean up after them, then you need to develop structures to help every employee or member identify *potential* problems as well as those that have already occurred. These structures need to be in place from the front lines up through senior management and the board. Everyone in the organization also needs to know exactly what to do if they observe either a problem or potential problem, whether in themselves or others.

3. Clear and Enforceable Procedures
for Dealing with Red Flags and Violations

Lest it need to be said, reducing the impact of ethics problems does not mean covering them up! It means intervening immediately and appropriately, conducting as thorough, effective, and discrete an investigation as possible, cooperating with law enforcement and government oversight as needed and to the greatest degree required by both the law and good citizenship, and using the information gathered in your investigation to further strengthen your ethics program. To the greatest possible extent, make it a quality improvement process as much as a compliance and disciplinary process. As with so many other issues in life, if you can't learn from your mistakes, you will be doomed to repeat them forever.

The above may be among the easiest things to learn how to do and yet many companies either overlook it entirely or provide only minimal training on it. All employees need to know at least the basics of how and when to confront others – and themselves – regarding ethics concerns, the do's and don'ts of consulting on ethics matters, to whom to report any concerns as well as any re-lated guidelines for doing so, and how to access supports (whether on the job or in the community) to deal with the kinds of personal issues that so often set the scene for ethics problems on the job.

In fairness, many companies and associations have recently beefed up their training on how and when to report ethics concerns – whether to supervisors, HR offices, compliance departments, or, sometimes, to the new wave of outsourced ethics hotlines. Too often, though, these efforts are all the training provided and effec-tive prevention and other intervention tools are not anywhere in the training picture.

Remember, even though prevention should always be your ultimate goal, assuming you will hit that mark every time is unrealistic. Inevitably, some problems – or, at the absolute very least, some observable *potential* for problems – will occur. Consequently, the measure of success is not whether problems or potential problems are found; it is how quickly you can spot them, how effectively you can deal with them, and how little impact they have on your organization. In the real world, the best one can realistically do is to prevent all the problems you reasonably can and then be fully equipped to deal with any emerging problems quickly and appro-priately enough that they do not create the legal, financial, and public relations nightmares to which ethics problems so frequent-ly lead. However, none of this will even begin to be possible until both your policies and procedures, in concert with your organiza-tional culture, make it so.

4. Clarity That Ethical Behavior Is a Cornerstone of Your Business Practices

This, of course, starts with your company's ethics and values statements. It also requires a good, hard look at how your entire management structure can model, encourage, and reinforce ethical decision-making. Though the use of performance appraisals for this reinforcement might seem like a great idea, remember that the best learning occurs when behavior is reinforced clearly and immediately after the desired behavior occurs. Because performance appraisals typically occur only once or perhaps twice per year, consider what you can do to provide clear and powerful reinforcement for appropriate behavior in a more immediate and effective manner.

Also remember that modeling and rewarding exceptional behavior – as opposed to simply rewarding the following of the rules – is important. You may well be able to combine this with other workforce improvement or customer-service initiatives. You need not label it as an ethics or values-improvement initiative unless you choose to. Simply find ways to make it clear that good, ethically attuned decisions – however you choose to define or label them – are both valued and encouraged. Also emphasize that such behavior directly supports your company's strongly held values. Remember, this will help foster your organization's team sense (e.g. "We're all in this together!") while simultaneously providing a fresh focus on the value of ethics and the long-term success that comes from a business based on clear, explicit values.

Improved Ethics Require More Than New Policies

Besides the creation of policies and procedures related to ethics improvement and monitoring, your company or association must also develop a culture in which employees or members feel comfortable reporting ethics concerns. For example, telling employees that they need to report concerns to a supervisor, compliance officer, or ethics officer does little good if they feel vulnerable to a retaliatory response. And remember, just because Federal laws protect whistle-blowers does not mean that employees know about or fully trust those protections. That only comes through persistent, effective training and the development of a culture in which management has earned the maximum possible trust. Everyone in the organization needs to know that management will handle all complaints promptly, fairly, thoroughly, and with the greatest possible discretion. Once that is established, assurances of non-retaliation are much more likely to be taken seriously.

Some senior executives have proudly told me about their survey statistics showing that eighty-something to ninety percent of their employees would feel comfortable reporting a perceived ethics violation in the workplace. Their pride may be somewhat justified given that so many companies have obtained survey results showing that only forty to sixty percent of their employees would feel comfortable taking such action. However, even though one always likes to look good compared to others, is an eighty-something to ninety percent reporting rate really all that terrific?

Of course, human nature will always create some unknown percentage of employees who, for whatever reasons, will be uncomfortable reporting inappropriate behavior. Consequently, there is no known, specific benchmark regarding what an acceptable percentage should be. On the other hand, it feels alarming that companies feel proud when a full ten percent or more of their employees would refrain from reporting clearly inappropriate behavior!

Management at all levels needs training not only on the policies regarding the appropriate response to ethics problems but also on how to create a climate in which addressing ethics issues is a strong value in itself. In other words, they need help in assuring that ethics are a prized and central value rather than an afterthought to the broader management agenda. We will discuss this idea a bit more in Chapters 8 and 9.

Think of this process like any other initiative you want to incorporate into your company's practices. You start with a goal (e.g. "Ethics will be a cornerstone of our practices."), define your terms (e.g. "These are the values of this company."), assure that the implemented processes are do-able (e.g. "Develop clear and enforceable mandates for behavior."), and establish a system to assure thorough, appropriate, and persistent follow-through. Then be sure to implement this process in every department and division in the organization.

Once done, you will have achieved a couple of very significant objectives. The first is that you will have set the tone for the cultural changes required to assure the most bulletproof ethics you can create. The second is that taking these steps, in and of themselves, will assure a greater focus on prevention and early intervention approaches to your employees' ethics challenges. That prevention and early intervention focus is, of course, the very foundation of how best to avoid the ethics disasters you never see coming.

Are the Basics Enough?

Building and maintaining better ethics is an on-going task so the basics are a starting point and not more. However, if you do nothing more than follow the four guidelines outlined in this chapter you will have already made a significant, running start towards reducing your organization's risk for ethics problems. That, by extension, should be also be extremely valuable in reducing your financial and legal risks as well. However, in addition, I hope that it also improves your sleep due to some reduced anxiety over potential ethics problems, both imagined and not.

Clearly, the ideas outlined in this chapter are easier said than done. However, you *can* do each one. In fact, you can without a doubt initiate every one of them today. Why not start right now by jotting down some notes about what you can do by the end of today, the end of this week, the end of this month, and the end of this quarter? (Appendix F will help you with this process.) Then hold yourself to those plans and you will be surprised how far you can get as well as how quickly you can get there.

Chapter Nine

Just Say No to
Just Saying No

The time is always right to do what is right.
– Martin Luther King, Jr.

We overlook one essential organizational cultural change so often that I have given it this chapter to itself. That cultural change involves creating the shift from seeing ethics as entirely prohibitive to seeing them as being equally a matter of permissions.

For some reason, we have come to think of ethics exclusively as the things we should not do. Certainly one of ethics codes' critical roles is to delineate the boundaries between right and wrong. Compliance and oversight programs, in turn, make sure no one has crossed those boundaries. However, we need to embrace a broader view of ethics if they are going to maximally assist in building stronger and more productive companies, schools, and associations. The problem is this; a disproportionate number of ethics codes are simply a list of what you are not supposed to do.

But what happens in companies who really encourage employees to do the right thing? I doubt they say, "You'll be great employees if you don't break the rules." After all, observing the rules ought to be the minimum expected behavior when you come in the door each morning!

I would suggest that taking initiative and personal responsibility are less likely to occur in organizations where management simply tells employees what they cannot do. After all, such an approach neither asks employees to think much nor does it inspire them in any way, shape or form – it simply boxes them in. Why not use the same amount of time and energy it takes to tell them what they cannot do to show them, instead, how to make great pro-active and responsive decisions all day long for their customers and your business?

Remember, as mentioned earlier, that effectively empowering your employees to make a wider range of decisions requires, among other things, that they know – as precisely as possible – who their customer is. Will that customer be the same for everybody in your company? Probably not. The people on the front-line must focus primarily or exclusively on the customer or task immediately in front of them. As you move up the supervisory and management chain, however, multiple customers will exist and, therefore, multiple and often contradictory expectations will come into play (i.e. the needs of the front-line and/or external customer vs. various other departments and divisions vs. the board vs. the shareholders, etc.). Knowing exactly who your customer is, as exactly as possible, will be essential to providing those customers with the best possible service.

Pay careful attention to where differing customer expectations and needs might lead one set of employees' mandates to overshadow or override another's; this becomes more of a risk as the number of simultaneous customer types become involved. When you notice that employees could get contradictory messages about who their customer is – and therefore how to answer service-related questions, ethical as well as otherwise – step in to clarify as soon as possible. Unless someone can tell them how to somehow meet both sets of contradictory expectations without compromising either of the two, you owe them, your company, and your customers some quick and clear direction.

An inconsistent message about the identity of the customer creates not only a threat to ethics, but also a threat to the effectiveness and profitability of your entire business. After all, if different segments of your organization are not coordinated regarding who they serve and why, how well-oiled can your organizational machine be? This does not mean that everyone needs to answer to the exact same type of customer(s) or in the exact same way– that would be close to impossible in any but the very smallest companies. It does mean, though, that the rationale for any disparities involving which customers get treated differently than others needs to be clear and the impact of inconsistent priorities minimized in any way possible. The bottom line here is that every individual in the organization needs to know to whom they are both directly and indirectly responsible, as well as what values and behaviors are required to meet the standard of customer-friendliness and customer service you expect for their particular constituency.

Simply getting this part right (e.g. "To whom is each individual responsible and what does that responsibility entail?") might require some system-wide evaluation and training. However, for efficiencies sake, you can probably build this into other customer service initiatives, especially for workers on or near the front lines since their jobs are usually less complicated in this particular area.

What might you ask of your front-line workers and their immediate managers? Probably things like really owning their customers' problems. And when training them to do so, you can easily and simultaneously help build an environment in which personal responsibility in general is mandated, valued, modeled and, conspicuously reinforced as well. This, then, helps ensure better customer service while setting the stage for improved ethics in the same stroke.

Here is another angle that I believe deserves very careful consideration. It seems to me that it is difficult to learn how to really think ethically until given the authority – if not the mandate – to make a real difference in the experience of others. In other words, it is tough to learn how to do good when one has no authority to do anything other than follow a set of rules. That approach simply breeds passive compliance rather than creating an environment in which employees are expected and able to go above and beyond merely following the rules. Sure, you can encourage them to smile and be polite while following the rules and that may improve their customers' experience. But to provide a fundamentally more powerful customer experience, your employees need to be able to do things that go beyond the mere routine and they cannot do that until allowed, trained, and encouraged to do so.

Once employees are making real decisions, a whole other layer or two of opportunities for ethical choices will emerge. Whether you feel that is a good thing or not is up to you, of course. However, I would argue that it is far more likely to be a very good thing as long as those employees have the training and oversight required to be persistently successful at taking on that new level of responsibility. It will make them a much more active and productive member of your team while allowing them to truly wow your customers at every turn.

By contrast, and from a strictly psychological perspective, if employees feel powerless in their job – if they have all responsibility and no authority – they are far more likely to act in self-serving ways just to feel more powerful (i.e. "No one else is looking out for me so I better look out for myself"). In turn, such self-serving attitudes are among the most potent breeding grounds for exactly the kinds of inappropriate behaviors that repeatedly spawn ethics and legal problems. Besides, if employees are only told what they cannot do, it is simply human nature to focus on, "Okay then, what *can* I do?" (i.e. "I know what this job takes – or what I want – better than the people making the rules do. I'm going to make sure it's done the way *I* like!"). In other words, it is an open invitation to look for loopholes and engage in inappropriate behavior simply because it is not explicitly prohibited.

To alleviate this, you need to nurture opportunities for individuals at every level of your organization to say "yes" as much as they are required to say "no." As mentioned previously, even if this did not improve employees' commitment to ethical behavior, it would still be a terrific shot in the arm for your customer service, staff relationships, and probably staff retention. So really, how can you lose with this approach?

Just remember, simply handing employees the ability to start saying "yes" is neither helpful nor fair. You must also provide clear information on the boundaries of their personal range of control, what to do if/when they reach the limits of that range, and real-world tools for effectively and ethically handling the situations for which they will now take responsibility.

Once accomplished, though, you will have simultaneously taken a huge set of steps toward better customer service (And whose bottom line isn't helped by that?) and towards your employees consistently taking the high road ethically.

When Personal Values Clash with Organizational Values

"We are here on earth to do good for others.
What the others are here for, I don't know."

– W. H. Auden

Most employees will ultimately act according to their personal values should there be a significantly large or otherwise intolerable conflict between their ethics and values and those of your organization. The degree to which this creates a risk for ethics problems, however, will largely be determined by how well your business can anticipate those potential clashes and then deal with them in a simultaneously sensitive and effective manner.

Looking at Values Clashes From a Management Perspective

The good news is that unless the difference between an employees' personal values and your organization's values are extremely large or truly and persistently jarring, most will stay with you, work their hardest to meet your business' objectives, and live by your organization's values and rules. Most of us actually tolerate such differences in personal versus organizational values pretty well unless we feel that we are betraying some truly fundamental personal value or are being asked to passively condone unethical or illegal behavior.

With the occasional worrisome exception, this leaves two small and rather opposite groups with a higher than average potential to either damage or leave your organization because of a clash of values. The first is made up of those very few employees who are truly criminally-minded and, hopefully, they will exit your organization as soon as possible, whether because of getting arrested, being terminated, or both. The second group consists of those equally few who will leave your organization at some point because they cannot tolerate some aspect(s) of how you do business. Certainly this latter group is of relatively little worry, at least as long as you take the time to be sure that their concerns are essentially differences in taste and/or working style and that their complaints are without merit as far as your organization's ethics. (In other words, make sure you learn from them everything you can. They will sometimes have extremely valuable feedback that was not said or, perhaps, was said but not heard until they decided to leave.) [15]

Here is the best way I know to minimize the size of each of these already-small groups. Think about what you can do to develop a partnership with your employees – *all* of your employees – in the development and maintenance of a culture of ethics. Consider how powerful it would be if your entire organization fully bought into the organizational values because they were able to see those values as a path towards their own success and not just yours. It is

---

[15] It is, of course, the worrisome exceptions mentioned at the beginning of this paragraph with whom much of this book is intended to deal. These are the otherwise good employees or association members who get pulled into some type of illegal or unethical behavior and either do not know it because they have not been trained to do things the proper way, do not notice it because they have not been appropriately trained on how to self-monitor, or do not know what to do to stop themselves once they have crossed the line. These folks will presumably represent a small group but unfortunately, the legal and financial risk they represent to your business cannot be overestimated.

a pretty simple idea – like most in this book – and yet it is one to which I rarely see companies attend. [16]

Creating this type of partnership with employees can be tough but it is certainly possible. To start this process you must be able to make a crystal clear and compelling case that every employee profits – whether literally, figuratively, or both – by doing the right thing (e.g. acting in a manner that fulfills the promise of your values statement). Of course, when I say that you need to make this pitch compelling, a part of what I mean is that it needs to be honest! Employees are quick to see when management's talk about any kind of partnering is a line of garbage. Following this, remember that it will also be helpful to make clear that abiding by your company's ethics and values is a significant part of being an accepted member of the team. (The trick sometimes, of course, is to be a more desirable "team" to join than that of any detractors you may have within the company…)

Here is another essential component of this approach that, to my perpetual amazement, seems to be easily to forgotten. Positive *or* negative, your behavior as a manager or executive sets the tone for everyone on your team – no matter how big or small your team and no matter how straightforward or complex its agenda or staffing. Be careful what you model! Not only must you communicate what you want your employees' values and behaviors to be but you had better be prepared to model those values and behaviors all day, every day as well. You cannot reasonably expect them to buy into mandates for their behavior that you cannot clearly buy into as well.

---

[16] Schools and associations have traditionally been well ahead of the curve on this one, by the way. They have long seen the value of common goals, common values, and various types of rallying cries into which the vast majority of their employees, members, or students can buy. These are framed in ways that show how 'joining the club' leads to personal or professional success. The corporate world could learn a number of significant lessons from how they do this.

The bottom line here is that partnering with employees around ethics and values will never happen – certainly not in a meaningful way or for long – if you are not seen as living and working according to the values by which you say you are expecting them to work. If they perceive you as tolerant of bending the rules or as willing to compromise your own stated values to get ahead, they will be far less likely to expend the energy required to conform their behavior to your stated ethical standards. After all, if you are loose with your ethics in any way, they can easily rationalize doing the same thing when it helps them, like you, to be successful in some real or perceived way. They are simply acting like you – their chosen model.

Positive *or* negative, your behavior sets the tone for your team. You need to model appropriate values and behavior all day, every day!

Looking at Values Clashes From an Employee Perspective

At some point in your career, you are likely to encounter a situation where you feel that management is acting in a manner either contrary to your personal values or contrary to the values that the organization is claiming to champion. Here are some guidelines for how to reduce the impact of those clashes when they occur:

1. If the clash is between your values and those of your company, consider how you might most effectively advocate for the company to reconsider its position. Depending on your role and perhaps your level of political skills or clout, you may be more or less successful with this kind of advocacy. However, consider giving it a try no matter what

you believe your chances of success may be.[17] Successful or not and frustrating or not, you are probably likely to feel better for having given it your best shot. Plus – and for your peace of mind, you need to remember this if at all possible – even if you see no immediate evidence of success, you may well have 'planted the seed' for changes that will occur in the future due to your efforts.

2. Think about whether or not the clash is due to your company's values actually being repugnant to you. The alternative is that their values are simply not what you would choose personally and this is a critical differentiation. You can probably tolerate many differences in values quite easily if they merely represent inconsistencies between your chosen focus or priorities and theirs. After all, we do this kind of tolerating in life all the time in everything from friendships to politics, and more. On the other hand, if you feel that your company's values are actually reprehensible and you cannot reasonably expect to change them, then you may well need to consider leaving. (See "*When Is Enough Of A Clash Enough?*" below.)

3. If you perceive a clash between others' behavior and your organization's stated values, then that is a time to put the ideas from the last section of Chapter 7 ("*What Else Can You Do*") into practice. Many of those ideas will apply to dealing with values clashes equally as well as they do to

---

[17] This is certainly one of the places where exercising appropriate tact and diplomacy can be invaluable. Remember, your ideas are far less likely to be taken seriously if delivered in an off-putting or unrelenting manner. You are, hopefully, trying to send a message suggesting some type of organizational self-evaluation, not be some kind of bully. And, if you feel so strongly about your concerns that tact is somehow beyond you, see whether what is written in section #2 is more relevant to your situation.

dealing with the discovery of an ethics problem. Should you become aware of such a clash, it will be important, at the very least, to speak up about your concerns to the proper individuals, regardless of how little or much authority you personally have to remedy the problem. As with any issue, keeping it to yourself cannot possibly affect positive change.

Once in a while, however, what appears to be a clash of values actually turns out to be an issue involving some type of previously unidentified unethical or illegal behavior. Lest it need to be said yet again, if you become aware of any type of illegal or unethical behavior, you need to immediately bring it to the attention of the appropriate person, department, or body responsible for oversight.

When Is Enough of a Clash Enough?

If at some point you encounter behavior in your organization's management that is simply ethically unacceptable to you, how can you best decide whether to advocate for change or just leave, whether hurriedly or otherwise? Before seriously considering leaving, I hope you will make every reasonable effort to assist in assuring that the inappropriate behavior is corrected. Chances are, you will have more power to correct the problem than you imagine; or, at the very least, to point out the problem to those who can and will assure that the proper corrections are made.

If the changes are not made, though, it would be understandable for you to want to leave. After all, no one wants to be associated with wrong-doing. Before you make that decision, though, you may want to consider the following:

1. If you have appropriately documented both the problem and your efforts to intervene – and let the appropriate supervisors, officers, law enforcement, or oversight providers

know about the problem – you have discharged your ethical duty. Your personal integrity should not be open to question simply by virtue of having worked for others known to lack such integrity. There is certainly always some risk of 'guilt by association' but this may be less of a risk than you imagine. Chances are, if it even affects your reputation at all, that you will be better known for correcting the problem than for having been negatively associated with it.

2. Remember that you are more likely to be able to promote change in your organization from the inside than from the outside. If positive organizational changes remain your goal, you may wish to stay as long as you reasonably can in order to maximize your potential to help create the changes you feel need to be made. If you leave, there is a good chance that you will lose any power you now have to see those changes through.

3. A strictly practical matter... It is almost always easier to get a job while employed so if you can at least wait until you have something else to move to, that may be better for you both personally and professionally. Of course, this in no way means that you should stay any longer than feels ethically correct. Still, though, there may not be a need to leave *today* unless there are truly dire circumstances.

4. Ultimately of course, only you can decide whether to stay, to leave now, or to leave later. For better or worse, there is no absolutely right or wrong decision, assuming that your continued presence does not cause an ethical problem for you in itself. (In which case, leaving is probably the only reasonable thing to do.)

If you think that staying and leaving can both be supported ethically, trust your gut and the degree to which you can or cannot sleep at night. If staying feels either dangerous to your career or poisonous to your soul, that is all you need to know about it being time to say 'enough is enough' and get out of there as quickly as you reasonably can.

Writing a Clash-Reducing Values Statement

As I hope has been made clear, there is plenty of room in organizations for differences between personal and organizational values and sometimes there is even room for some pretty big differences. The trick, regardless of whether you are a front-line employee or a member of management, is to deal with those differences in a manner unlikely to set the stage for ethics problems.

As an employee, this usually means refraining from dealing with any values clashes by passive-aggressive or outright contrarian or sabotaging behavior as some form of retaliation. As a manager or executive, it means handling such clashes with appropriate tact, diplomacy, and open-mindedness. If your employees have strong feelings about values that you may be neglecting, give them a listen. You may well not end up agreeing with them but paying attention to their feedback is critical; aside from helping to build a partnering relationship, you never know when you will hear something terribly important that would otherwise have been overlooked.

Another of your best tools for preventing damaging fallout from values clashes is the writing of a well-conceived and fully enforced ethics code and values statement. Done correctly, these documents will explicitly allow for a diversity of opinions while making absolutely clear what employees' core values and behavior must be while on the job.

To do this, it will be important for your organization to write ethics and values statements able to speak clearly and effectively to all of your employees or members. After all, your ethics or values statement will be far less useful if segments of your employee or member population cannot understand, relate to, or agree to it.

When developing these documents, it will be helpful to solicit feedback from throughout your organization because you will want to hear and consider how your organization's values are currently understood and applied. Not only might this help you to identify some important values to which you had not previously attended, but this is essential information for management to have for all kinds of other reasons as well. It is tough to nurture a values-driven organization unless you know that everyone actually understands your values! And if they do not understand your organization's values, you had better learn how those values have been misunderstood so that you can provide the corrective information.

Lest it need to be said, even though you should be gathering this feedback, it is your leadership – and not your total organization – that needs to be responsible for deciding what your department's, division's, or organization's values and behavioral expectations will be. Partnering does not mean that management is somehow beholden to the current values of your front-line employees; they are still working for your company and not the other way around! The point is that care needs to be taken to understand and consider as many points of view as you can. Once done, you will be better able to conceptualize and state your values and behavioral expectations, to the greatest degree possible, in a manner able to be easily understood and put into practice by everyone in your organization.

Fortunately, soliciting feedback from throughout your organization does not need to mean ending up with one of the atrocities created when writing a 'document by committee'. Nor does it require 'dumbing down' the content for the sake of being understood by a wider range of readers. In fact, the latter will be a disaster if it compromises these documents' range or depth. Instead, these documents simply need to clearly and cleanly articulate your values, and the kinds of behavior you expect, in terms that are easily understood by whoever will need to abide by them. This may require some skilled conceptualizing and, perhaps, some talent at both writing and editing. It is, however, entirely possible to create such documents; you just need to keep clearly in mind what you are after in terms of both the style and content.

In recent years, more and more companies have turned the writing of their ethics and values statements over to corporate counsel. These counsels have, in turn, created legalistic sounding documents geared more towards risk management than either clarity or informed buy-in by employees. These are often extremely well crafted documents from a legal standpoint – they just do not to fulfill their intended purpose of clarifying and inspiring your desired or required values and behavior because, among other things, almost no one can actually understand them.

This is in no way meant to diminish the importance of risk management, which is obviously a significant matter that companies cannot even think about ignoring. However, once an ethics or values statement starts sounding more like a legal document and less like a clear, straightforward affirmation of your values, how easily or comfortably can everyone in your organization actually adopt and embrace it? The more technical the tone, the more likely it is that your employees will not understand the language, be put off by the style, or, in a few other awkward cases, be so enamored with the "legalese" that they miss the actual intended spirit of what you are trying to say!

Do what you can to make your ethics and values statements clear, direct, and conversational. Also, the more brief it is, the better because you want to make it as easy as possible to remember. The bottom line? Make these documents easy to comprehend, recall, and apply. A model for this type of document is provided in Appendix E.

Does it make sense to run your ethics and values statements past corporate counsel for review? Certainly. Hopefully they can help fine-tune some of your ideas. Just remember that counsel's feedback need not change the tone or style of your final statement. You are, after all, writing a document to which people at all levels of your organization will need to relate, not just your legal advisors. (Should you need additional risk management documents as well, they will certainly point that out to you and help you create them.)

Once you have created a solid and accessible ethics and values statement, follow up with the creation of a corporate posture fully imbued with clear, compelling, and indelible methods for getting buy-in from front-line employees right up through the board of directors. This will involve training and, above all, conspicuous modeling and persistent reinforcement of the values you desire employees to use as the foundation for their work.

Regardless of the diversity of opinions, personal styles, and personal values held by your employees or association members, you need to do anything you can to find wording around which everyone can really rally. Again, if significant segments of your employees or members cannot relate to the stated values of the organization – or if they see that the stated values are not really what management practices – that is, at best, an open invitation to feelings of alienation. And, of course, alienation is a terrific foundation for all kinds of unethical and illegal behavior.

Create ethics and values statements in a style that allows easy understanding and maximum buy-in from all employees. This doesn't mean 'dumbing them down.' It just means making them clear and easy to adopt.

Chapter Eleven

Special Challenges for Managers, Executives, and Boards

"He who would move the world must first move himself."

– Edward Ericson

Whether at the level of the office, work-group, department, division, or corporation, those in charge must model and encourage appropriate behavior. That is hopefully a given. After all, leaders carry the greatest responsibility for setting the tone for both ethics and compliance.

Yet, we see just as many ethics breaches in leadership as anywhere, and some would argue that leaders are even *more* susceptible to ethics lapses. Some version of "power corrupts" is the usual explanation but remember, those in charge also have more overall latitude for key decision-making. Therefore, they may have more opportunities to make not more but, rather, more conspicuous bad choices as well as good ones. (And, of course, in some cases unfortunately, power actually *does* corrupt.)

Whether or not leaders are more prone to make quantitatively or qualitatively worse decisions, the fact remains that leaders need to consistently model and encourage the most ethically appropriate decisions and behaviors possible. As discussed previously, this process ought to include the development of rock-solid ethics and values statements with which everyone will be expected to comply.[18]

In addition, leaders must constantly find effective ways to encourage ethical thinking in others and help set up systems through which managers and executives will notice and reward ethical behavior. Certainly, this cannot take the place of time and effort spent assuring the efficiency and effectiveness of audit and compliance systems. After all, you will always need those systems and other controls, even if the law did not require them.

As stated previously, however, if your organization is relying on audit and control functions as your front-line, primary effort to build an ethically attuned culture, you are missing the ethics boat by miles and miles. Why? Because you are still putting your primary efforts, resources, and priorities regarding ethics into the detection and remediation of ethics problems that already exist rather than preventing those problems from occurring in the first place. This approach represents the traditional culture of compliance versus truly representing a culture of ethics.

Managers, executives, and board members obviously also have other special obligations for upholding organizations' ethics. Besides simply setting the tone, they also have a greater responsibility for developing and fine-tuning initiatives assuring that the organizational culture fully supports its espoused ethics and values. That is simply a part of the job.

In addition though, as an executive or board member, of course you also carry a much larger burden from a legal standpoint. After

---

[18] Although the complete process of creating these documents is beyond the scope of this book, both Appendix A and Appendix E provide some basic ideas with which to start. In addition, Appendix D provides a highly effective model for conceptualizing a 'starter set' of foundations and initiatives necessary to develop a department, division, or organization-wide culture of ethics.

all, you sign off on all the documents that will be scrutinized by external auditors, the IRS, and anyone who happens to be suing the organization at the moment. It is no secret that you have a more direct, personal liability for wrongdoing than others in the management chain. Even if you did not directly contribute to someone else's lapse in judgment or behavior, the stark reality is that if it happens on your watch, in your chain of command, and under your signature, you will often hold a significant degree of personal liability. You may or may not consider this the least bit fair but, fair or not, it is unquestionably the reality in today's version of organizational accountability.

As those most responsible for ethics oversight, executives and other senior managers should never underestimate the impact of poor judgment or inappropriate behavior on the front lines. You may think, "That employee holds a pretty insignificant job so any violation there will have a small impact," or "Those are problems for lower level managers to take care of because it really doesn't affect anyone above their level." As will be discussed in the next chapter, both of these ways of thinking can be extremely dangerous.

Regardless of where in the organization an ethics lapse occurs, top company or association officials must address them. This does not mean that senior managers must somehow be directly involved in every detail within their chain of command. It does mean, though, that they need to be aware of what types of difficulties are occurring so as to be able to assure the correction of those problems through appropriate oversight, training, or both.

In addition, managers at *every* level need the training and authority to recognize and remediate ethics problems created anywhere in their respective chains of command. They will need both the encouragement and the resources to develop effective prevention and early intervention initiatives for the areas over which they have responsibility. Further, they should be empowered to initiate such initiatives as promptly as they see fit because if they need to wait for a coordinated company-wide program, they may lose the many advantages of striking while the proverbial iron is hot.

Despite the increased legal exposure of managers, executives, and board members, their best methods for effective self-monitoring are identical to everyone else's. That is simply because the concepts, tools, and techniques for effective self-monitoring have to do with personal values, perceived personal needs, and personal experience as opposed to job descriptions.

Unfulfilled needs for status, money, friendship, or approval; difficulties with sticking out one's neck to confront co-workers or other types of assertiveness issues; difficulty setting appropriate limits on one's behavior or the behavior of others; mental health or substance abuse issues; relationship issues, etc., are common ethics risk factors associated with nothing more than being human. They are no more or less likely to occur in the cleaning crew as in the chair of the board. The key to reducing these risk factors' potential negative impact, regardless of one's title or job description, is knowing how these issues – or how ignoring them – can set the scene for unethical behavior. That knowledge must then be used to both identify and mitigate the risks created by those issues, as completely as is possible and as immediately as is possible, no matter who you are or what your job might be.

Managers', executives' and board members' risk factors and required self-monitoring techniques are identical to everyone else's. That is because once you know the rules, ethics lapses typically stem from personal issues that are no different for employees at the top of your organization as anywhere else.

Chapter Twelve

Whose Ethics Really Matter?

If each one sweeps before his own door,
the whole street is clean.

– Yiddish Proverb

Most of us are quick to appreciate the potential negative impact of unethical behavior on the part of managers and executives. However, for some reason we are easily seduced into thinking that 'lower level' employees do not have anywhere near the same potential to hurt the real or perceived integrity of our companies. However, just because an employee does not have a high-powered title does not mean that they cannot cause some serious financial or reputational damage to your organization through their illegal or unethical behavior. Everyone's ethics matter!

Here are two quick examples of very different kinds of problems that can occur when not everyone at every level is fully a part of your ethics team:

A company with whom I worked had an 'informal policy' that senior management, other than HR, need not be notified about petty theft because, after all, "It was only a couple of dollars here and there and certainly not the kind of thing worth the time of higher level managers." They failed to appreciate that all those 'couples of dollars here and there' were rapidly adding up to hundreds of thousands of lost dollars. In the meantime, the managers who were directly supervising the employees on the front lines were unwilling to confront the thieving workers on what was clearly embezzlement. Meanwhile, those front-line staff certainly felt no incentive to confront one another because they were taking in money hand-over-fist and saw their managers' lack of intervention as tacit approval.

Had higher level managers chosen to take seriously the presence of ethics problems along their full chain of command, not only could the company have saved a great deal of money, but they also could have prevented the development of an entire culture of thievery in one of its wings. The aftermath of that culture's development took many years to fully erase.

As another example, a few years ago I prepared a seminar on ethics self-monitoring for the regional division of a large national association. A member of the meeting planning team – certainly not someone considered 'high level' by those outside the organization – used the association's mailing list to send an email that, although somewhat ambiguous, was interpreted by many recipients as bigoted. In their minds it encouraged distrust and dislike of members of a certain ethnicity and religion.

Although this staff person was immediately fired, the damage had already been done. Not only did she offend a number of association members, but her inappropriate actions made it appear, however inaccurately, that the organization allowed loose cannons to work there. Even despite the regional president's immediate and heartfelt apology, a number of members resigned their long-standing membership from the local chapter, and in some cases, from the national organization as well.

Think of it this way: the integrity of your company is being judged all day, every day on the basis of *everyone's* behavior, from the person answering the phone all the way up to the top. And who

actually interacts more with your customers and potential customers; is it the receptionist answering the phone or your senior
management? Is it your vice president for sales or the front-line
sales person making their sales calls all day, every day? Unless
your business is dramatically different than most, I can promise
you that the person answering the phone or the salesperson on the
phone or street has significantly more contact with your customers
than anyone else further up the chain of command.

So, who has the most opportunity to do or say something that
might lead a customer or potential customer to question your
company's integrity? My money says it will be the receptionist,
salesperson – or anyone else acting as a front-line 'face' for your
organization – pretty much every time. Yet, are they ever actually
trained on the ethics and values of your organization and how best
to bring those values to life in the course of their day-to-day job
duties? Probably not, and I would suggest that it is a problem with
the potential to be a significant one.

Think of it this way; when you check into a hotel and receive
lousy service, do you tell your friends and business associates
that it really was not actually a problem because, after all, you
know all about the hotel chain's executive management and they
are all great, customer service oriented people? I don't think so!
Instead, I would bet that you immediately tell your friends and
associates the kind of cranky/funny/disgusted stories we would
all tell in order to steer our friends and family clear of that hotel
in the future.

The potential impact of your employees' behavior is no different,
regardless of where they work in the hierarchy of your business.
If a customer, potential customer, or business associate hears a
comment or sees behavior showing a lack of regard for honesty
or fair practices, a distasteful bias of any kind, a lack of concern
for confidentiality or financial accuracy, etc., no matter who says

it and no matter what their role in your organization may be, some amount of damage is done.[19]

As discussed earlier, when compared to front-line employees, your higher-level managers and executives probably have the greatest opportunity to create financially significant errors as well as more damaging press because of their position in your company. However, the enormity of significant, cumulative damage able to be done elsewhere in your organization must not be overlooked.

The integrity of your business is being judged all day and every day on the basis of everyone's behavior, from the person answering the phone all the way up through senior management. Because of this, ethics and values need to be trained at *every* level of your organization.

---

[19] See Appendix B for just one of many examples of an ethics threat that can be simultaneously faced by multiple organizational levels and by employees in multiple types of jobs. This particular example – how to deal with incentives and inducements – was chosen among the many others because it is one faced by virtually every industry in one way or another.

Chapter Thirteen

No One Said the
High Road Would Always
Be an Easy Walk

*"Sometimes, the hardest decision made
is the right thing to do."*

– Yanny Natashah

Wouldn't it be nice if life always allowed us our deepest beliefs without being required to make tough choices about
where, when, and to which degree we are morally obligated to
express them? In the real world, though, we must take a firm stand
from time to time and some of us must do so more often than others. Sometimes that stand is difficult to take because of some real
or imagined risk involved with speaking out. Unfortunately, those
fears may be quite realistic. However, our ability to rise to the
challenge of speaking our truth will determine our ability to take
the high road when the going gets tough. It will also determine
how well we can shine as a leader and positive role model.

Will taking that high road always be easy? Certainly not. However,
your willingness to stand by your beliefs and values, even in the
face of adversity, is at the core of maintaining solid ethics. Might
you lose some friends, money, or status in the eyes of those whose
beliefs you do not share? Maybe so. Will others always support
you in speaking out? No, though you will probably be supported
more frequently than you may imagine. Remember, if something is
an ethics or integrity concern for you, it probably concerns others

too and they will appreciate you taking a strong stand. In addition, most people deeply respect those willing to take a stand on their beliefs. Why not be that person?

No one likes discovering the hard way who their true friends and supporters are. Should you take an unpopular stand, you might not be as supported as you would like. But, if the choice is to for-ever avoid expressing your real convictions versus speaking up, I hope that the choice is easy and that you will choose to speak up. Whatever or whoever you lose because of taking your stand is likely counter-balanced by the better sleep you will get each night and by the pride you will feel each time you look in the mir-ror. Further, if you also support others in *their* willingness to take a stand, I suspect that your comfort level and personal pride will increase all the more.

When you see or hear something that conflicts with the law (in-cluding civil rights as well as financial irregularities, etc.), ethical business practices, or the expressed values of your company or as-sociation, speaking up as clearly and as immediately as possible is imperative. There is simply no excuse for doing otherwise.

Stick to Your Convictions

> *"These are my values and if you*
> *don't like them, I have more."*
>
> – Groucho Marx

Tales of corporate misdeeds are frequently riddled with mention of otherwise good people who just could not muster the nerve to take a stand against ethically inappropriate behavior. These individuals either feared for their job, their reputation, their income level, or the personal or business relationships they held dear. (Others, of course, saw wrongdoing and simply decided that joining in was more fun or more profitable. As mentioned earlier, however, such criminally-minded folks are actually the rare exception and not the rule.)

Among the reasons we have come to revere corporate whistle-blowers is that they model principles over profit or convenience. That can be an extremely tough stance for many of us, especially if we perceive a dollar or status cost for speaking out. Even the powerful federal protections guaranteed to whistle-blowers are not enough for many people to conjure up whatever it takes to stand by their convictions in the face of a prospectively turbulent reaction. However, seeing a wrong being done and not acting to correct it creates both ethical and legal culpability. Inaction is simply unacceptable.

Be clear about your convictions and be prepared to stand by them. You will feel a whole lot better when willing to speak up for what you truly believe. Might the impact of your statements be best served by the use of accurate, diplomatic language and by appropriately choosing your audience? Certainly. Those needing to be confronted or informed of your concerns will be much more likely to take you seriously if you are tactful and if the apparent accuracy of your comments is unassailable. Just remember that diplomacy means being totally honest in as tactful a way as you can; it is not an excuse for either inaccuracy or dishonesty.

Also, although diplomacy can be of terrific value, if you ever feel that your choice is between silence and duplicity or speaking up undiplomatically about ethics concerns, remember that the undiplomatic truth will always fare better than silence or dishonesty. Silence equals passive consent no matter how many ways you might try to spin it differently.

As for your choosing your audience, they should be the people who really need to hear that something inappropriate is taking place. Do not just discuss your concerns at the water cooler. Rather, present your concerns directly to those responsible for oversight and/or investigation. As obvious as that might sound, it is amazing how often ethics concerns languish in break-room discussions and are never taken to those who really need to be informed.

"That you may retain your self-respect,
it is better to displease people by doing what you know
to be right rather than temporarily pleasing them
by doing what you know to be wrong."

– William J. H. Boetcker

A Naïve View of Decision Making?

"Things refuse to be mismanaged long."

– Theodore Parker

People sometimes ask me whether I really believe that every individual will be willing or able to consistently focus on organizational values or ethical mandates in the course of day-to-day decision-making. I have been told that such an assumption is naïve. (This is typically offered in the same breath as a smirking comment that "business ethics" is actually an oxymoron). I do not buy that for a moment.

As an example, does anyone doubt that you or your employees or association members – from the front-lines up through senior managers and the board of directors – can learn to carry out required job duties while filtering the value or appropriateness of their behavior through your organization's mission statement? It is simply the expected thing to do. Why would it be any different to ask folks to filter their behavior through, say, your organization's ethics and values statements? I do not buy that there is a difference and believe that, given the motivation to do so, every single employee or member can do it.

Now I certainly agree that not all employees or members will use your values statement or ethics code as touchstones if those statements are too long and detailed to be remembered or if those employees or members do not have training or persistent reinforcement for putting an adequately easily-recalled ethics or values statement into use. But here again, how different is that from asking employees or association members to live by your mission statement? If leaders either do not model and reinforce that mission or effectively train and actively support employees or members in molding their behavior to support it, it probably will not happen all that often. Assuring adherence to your organization's values and stated ethics requirements is no different.

In promoting ethics, as with so many other aspects of your organization, leaders at all levels have an obligation, as well as endless opportunities, to model the behavior they expect of those they lead. Mandating a persistent and conspicuous effort to do so with ethics is nothing more than common sense.

Chapter Fourteen

Where From Here?

*"Act as if what you do makes
a difference. It does."*

– William James

The measure of success for this type of book is the degree to which it presents useful ideas that can be effectively and immediately put to use. With that goal in mind, let me leave you with a few reminders of key points as well as a few last minute new ideas – each presented here as a call to action. As you well know, it is up to you and no one else to start putting them into practice, hopefully remembering that now is the time to start and not later. To help get you going as well as to help you stay on task, Appendix F provides you with a place to start sketching out your implementation plan as well as key target dates.

Make Prevention a Priority

What does it take to make the prevention of ethics problems and early intervention a priority for everyone in your work-group, department, division, or entire organization? Like with any prospective initiative, start with creating the greatest possible buy-in at the top of whichever part of the organization you work. This will help assure a commitment of the resources required to develop appropriate training and oversight programs. Much more fundamentally, though, it will hopefully also assure that leaders are committing to an unyielding ethical standard in order for those under them to be effectively guided down the same path. It is not enough for leaders' buy-in to occur on paper alone; they must also be willing and able to consistently demonstrate their buy-in through their behavior.

Senior managers, executives, and boards need to envision an appropriate and enforceable ethics and values mandate upon which they can all agree and be willing to be held accountable. Then they need to help the rest of the organization join them in that same accountability. If you cannot create such a vision or implementation plan on your own, bring in someone who can help you with it. This is far too important a task to either take lightly or settle for a partially completed job. This mandate needs to clearly define the values (not just policies and procedures!) that you expect to be built into all business decisions of all employees at all times. Then you need to assure that you have the processes in place to assure that this is actually happening.

Remember, this mandate needs to say more than what employees cannot do. It also needs to provide explicit information on what employees can and need to do in order to bring the ethics code, code of conduct, and your organization's core values to life throughout each working day. In other words, it needs to empower and encourage at least as much as it restricts.

Next, review your ethics and values statements as well as your code of conduct. Do they fully and accurately represent the ethics and values you want to hold up as the cornerstone, defining principles of your company or association? If not, you need to articulate them more clearly and cleanly. This will also be a good time to make sure that you are actually stating your values and not simply your organization's slogans. If you are not sure about the difference between these, please refer to Appendix G.

Make every effort to bolster your internal oversight programs but at the same time, see if you can restructure the role of audit and compliance departments as they relate to the rest of the organization. Can you create opportunities for their wisdom and experience to be used in a more consultative role vis-à-vis the prevention of ethics problems as opposed to exclusively being used for their expertise with after-the-fact oversight and intervention? Because prevention will almost certainly cost less than cleaning up a mess allowed to develop or fester, why not harness the expertise of those audit and compliance professionals to make your preventive efforts as rock-solid as possible? You are already paying for their expertise, why not benefit as much from that expertise as you possibly can?

Provide the Necessary Training and Resources

Create training programs that give *all* employees the concepts and tools they need to bring the mandate of clean, transparent, business-promoting ethics and values to life. Remember that simply teaching the ethics code or corporate code of conduct is inadequate. Similarly, case studies – although they can often be extremely helpful – are also inadequate if used without additional kinds of training. Truly effective training will include opportunities for employees to identify their individual risk factors for ethics difficulties and specific techniques to effectively recognize, monitor, and mitigate those risks.

Study the availability and affordability of effective, accessible support services for employees. This includes employee assistance programs, high quality insurance coverage for physical and mental health issues, substance abuse treatment, child-care plans, wellness programs, financial planning services, savings opportunities, etc. Remember, ethics problems all-too-frequently start with emotional, financial, or health pressures unrelated to the job. If you can reasonably help reduce those pressures, then it seems logical that you will also reduce ethics risks accordingly[20].

Has this logic been proven? Not that I am aware of although I believe that someday it will be. However, even if you believe that this logic makes no sense – and, in fact, even if you argue that these types of employee supports simply open the door to benefit abuse – would you not agree that providing the maximum possible support for employees is highly likely to improve both morale and retention? And, if improved morale and retention are 'all' you get, aren't those extremely worthwhile benefits to your business in themselves?

Of course, even if you buy into this employee support concept, you may well be unable to afford a number of these perks for employees, regardless of how good your organization's intentions may be. After all, many employers these days have trouble enough just keeping up with the spiraling cost of healthcare benefits if they can even provide coverage at all.

You may need to make some very tough decisions about how much money you can realistically put into these types of employee supports. However, taking the time to carefully consider their potential value will possibly lead you to accomplish at two important side-tasks:

---

[20] Note that increasing salaries and other direct compensation have not been mentioned. If your company's salaries are equitable, there is no reason to believe that increased direct compensation, in itself, will reduce ethics problems. Otherwise, why would so many highly paid senior executives become embroiled in major ethics scandals? Regardless of their salary level, though, you can help employees at *all* income levels create more healthy and comfortable lifestyles using whatever their particular financial resources might be. This, in turn, should reduce some of the financial, health-related, and emotional pressures that underlie so many ethics problems.

1. It will require that you spend some time being thoughtful about the impact of employees' personal and work experience on their abilities to fulfill their employment obligations. This, in turn, may well set the stage for some effective brainstorming on novel ways to improve your employees' work experience. That thinking, in turn, has the potential to help you create a work environment where employees not only enjoy themselves more but – more to the point of this book – are more prone to take seriously their commitment to work effectively and efficiently as well as ethically. After all, just as we know that customers' experience significantly affects their willingness to do business with us on our terms, so is the case with your employees' experience on the job. This is far from a novel idea, of course; yet it is still one that far too few companies actually seem to think about.

2. It may provide an opportunity to brainstorm some interesting ideas for obtaining not only the types of supports mentioned here but others as well through new types of partnering or alliances, reallocation of resources, etc.

Remember, ethics violations – other than when committed strictly out of ignorance of what the right thing is to do – usually arise from issues *off* the job that are then played out in the workplace. Therefore, it just makes sense that an effective prevention program will include doing everything within reason to reduce the emotional, legal, financial, behavioral, and time management difficulties that so easily lead to ethics problems on the job. The goal here is not – and, in fact, should not – be to become some kind of dependency-creating caretaker for your employees. Rather, it is to become a partner with them, in whichever sane and affordable ways you can, to show that you are invested in them as you expect them to be invested in you, while at the same time reducing a number of the pressures that so often lead to ethics problems on the job.

Create Foolproof Feedback Systems

Be sure that everyone for whom you are managerially responsible – whether employee or contractor – has the required knowledge and motivation to immediately inform the correct person if they have concerns about *anyone's* ethics in the organization. Multiple options for reporting such a concern must exist in those feedback systems. For example, it makes no sense to mandate that ethics concerns should only be reported to one's boss because that boss might be the very person about whom the employee needs to make a report! Be sure to provide the greatest possible number of explicit and well-defined alternatives for responding to a known or suspected ethics problem.

Also remember, just because whistle-blowers have legal protections does not mean that everyone in your business will trust those protections. An additional complication can be that employees may feel that turning in a colleague, co-worker, or supervisor could be destructive either for themselves or to your organization. Not only might they might fear retribution, but they may also fear that a valued employee or friend will be lost if that other employee's problems are reported.

Focus on creating an environment in which everyone views feedback, both to co-workers and management, as just another part – in fact, a highly valued part – of getting the job done right. Most importantly, be sure to reinforce – as persistently and compellingly as possible – the idea that addressing questionable behavior makes for an all-around better organization. As a significant part of that message, work to frame ethics as a great tool for *everyone's* success.

Include Everyone

Remember that ethics problems can and do occur at every level of your organization – that is simply the reality. Therefore, ethics and values training also need to occur at every level as well.

Even though senior management and the board of directors have the most risk-imbued jobs, everyone in your organization has the potential to make mistakes in judgment or self-control. Those mistakes can have a huge negative impact on your business, regardless of who is responsible for them.

Right or wrong, perception is everything. If *anyone* in your organization says or does something that does not appear to be on the up-and-up when in sight or earshot of a customer or potential customer, it can all-too-easily affect that customer's willingness to do business with you. A marred reputation, regardless of who is doing the marring, can often equal opportunity cost. Of course, if your business' reputation is damaged due to a *proven* ethics violation, you might also be looking at fines and jail time on top of that opportunity cost. If nothing else does the trick, hopefully the combination of these risks will provide some significant motivation for your management team and board to keep a clear focus on building and maintaining great ethics at very level of your organization; the stakes are simply too high to do otherwise.

If you really want to manage risk effectively, though, do not just train one segment of your organization; train everyone. Where you start will, of course, depend on your jurisdiction as well as your particular needs, resources, and priorities. Once you start, though, do your very best to keep going until everyone under your management has been trained. Then be sure that they regularly review and update their training – annually is not too often.

Make It Personal

Work to build a stronger organization by uniting every one of your employees through shared ethics and values. But remember, the most important things you can do to improve your company's or association's ethics will never start or end with 'them'. They will always start and end with you. Period.

It is essential to hone, review, and promulgate well-articulated ethics policies and procedures as well as to create bulletproof compliance, governance, and oversight systems. However, in the end, it is the personal issues that you and everyone else in your organization brings to work each day that hold the greatest sway over whether you or they create or participate in your organization's next as yet unanticipated ethics disaster. Your willingness and ability to be conscious of those issues, as well as your willingness to both recognize and mitigate their risk, will determine just how able you are personally to avoid – and help your company or association avoid – the many potential ethics disasters that you would never otherwise have been able to see coming.

MAKE PREVENTION A PRIORITY
PROVIDE THE NECESSARY TRAINING AND RESOURCES
CREATE FOOLPROOF FEEDBACK SYSTEMS
INCLUDE EVERYONE
MAKE IT PERSONAL

Appendix A

Make Your Ethics Statement More Than a Statement

An ethics or values statement and a *credible* ethics or values statement are two very different things. If the statement is to be credible, the first, and paramount, step is for you and all of your organization's leadership to be sure that you are clearly, persistently, and visibly working by your stated values and ethics in all ways and at all times. If it is truly only a statement rather than being a written explanation of what you are actually doing and why, you are sunk.

The next step towards credibility is assuring that your ethics and values statements have the maximum buy-in from the front lines on up to the very top. Unfortunately, as with so many organizational mandates, ethics and values statements are usually written with little or no input from the majority of employees or members who are bound by them. In fact, even senior managers are often only indirectly involved. A great number of ethics and values statements are written by human resources departments and/or corporate counsel, perhaps with input from the board, and then passed through senior management for approval. Upon the approval of senior management, the statements are then handed down to the rest of the organization.

Ethics and values statements created and disseminated in this manner frequently appear to be jargon-filled risk management documents that, in their stilted legal language, do little to inspire understanding or interest in the very values they are intended to promote. The fact that they might be well written documents from a legal standpoint helps little if they cannot provide clarity and inspiration for your employees.

To create a more effective statement, solicit input from all levels of the organization, including as many front-line workers as possible. The goal is not to write a statement by committee as such documents are notoriously poorly written. Rather, the goal is to obtain the maximum relevant input into the document that, in turn, can provide the following significant advantages:

1.) Including employees from all levels will help to maximize buy-in. When they have input into ethics and values statements, as with the development of virtually any policy, they will probably feel more connected to it. Is this likely to make a significant change in the amount of buy-in? There is no good way to predict, however *any* additional buy-in will be helpful.

2.) Including a range of employees will help to create an additional conduit for essential feedback regarding how your organization's management and leadership are seen from the front lines. Find a method of soliciting comments on prospective ideas or drafts of the statements using questionnaires, focus groups, or any other approach that encourages uncensored feedback. If senior management really puts their values – and the proposed values for the entire organization – out for critique, you might be surprised by the kinds of comments you receive. You may well get some extremely valuable information about how your 'advertised' ethics and values do or do not compare with the realities of everyday operations at various levels of your organization. Finding that out will be extremely important, and you can then make any needed changes in your operations accordingly.

Appendix B

Incentives and Inducements

I am frequently asked how do decide whether or not to accept some kind of special offer, gift, or other item of value. This, it seems, is a question that cuts across almost every department in every industry. Managers deal with this question, as do boards of directors. Sales staff also deal with it as, of course, do buyers of all stripes.

More and more organizations deal with this issue by writing very explicit mandates as far as what is acceptable and what is not. This is often in the form of a blanket statement saying that no gift is acceptable from anyone with whom one has a business relationship. In some cases, that extends to anyone having a business relationship with any part of the company, even different departments or divisions. Other companies – as well as most government agencies – have quite explicit guidelines as far as the value or type of gift employees may accept.

Most of the business world, however, does not have a clear mandate on which to base decisions regarding the acceptance of goodies, whether merchandise, monetary incentives, trips, favors, etc. Here is my best shot at guidelines that will fit most people under most circumstances: An incentive is anything that adds value to an already good deal *for your customer*. In other words, an incentive is something that makes a good deal better. It could be a price break, additional value for the same money, opportunities to do other kinds of business at a genuinely better rate or of higher quality, etc. Again, a true incentive is value added. As a very general rule, the more clearly something qualifies as a value added item, the more likely you can accept it without ethical compromise[21].

Branded giveaways are, of course, one of the backbones of modern marketing. Do they influence your buying decisions? Those providing the giveaways certainly hope so! However, whether that influence is "undue" is something only your company or trade association can decide. That is because what is thought to exert influence – undue or not – in one field or industry may not always be considered to do so in another field or industry.

An inducement, however, is a different story, even though they can easily take the same outward appearance as an incentive or marketing giveaway. The difference is that, instead of adding value to an already good deal, an inducement increases the likelihood of your accepting something other than the best deal. Either it adds insufficient value to turn the offer into the best deal or, as is often the case, it is a perk for the prospective buyer and holds no actual value for the buyer's customer at all. The more an offer looks like an inducement rather that an incentive, the more likely it is to invite an ethical compromise if accepted. Again, the purchaser's customer – whether internal or external – reaps the benefit of an incentive but an inducement rewards the buyer or

---

[21] An entire class of incentives about which one needn't worry are the incentive systems used inside companies to reward effort or achievement. It's tough to think of any way in which such a system could present ethical difficulties as long as they are equitable across employees (e.g. there is no discrimination favoring certain classes of employees among those eligible), the incentives are actually attainable by those it is intended to encourage, and it does not give incentive to illegal or otherwise inappropriate transactions. Otherwise, risks only appear when accepting items from outside your organization that could unduly influence your business decisions.

buyer's department and reduces or simply ignores any benefit to the buyer's customer.

As exaggerated examples, no one would reasonably suggest that it is acceptable to buy a vote, a jury decision, the award of a contract, or favorable press in a presumably unbiased news source. However, these are really just extreme examples of inducement. Anytime you accept a trip, service, money or other gift from a vendor as a pre-offered payment for considering or delivering a sale, you have succumbed to an inducement. That is because you have been reinforced ("induced") to attend to *your* gain rather than the gain of your customer.

Is the difference between an incentive and an inducement always clear? Certainly not. How about expenses-paid educational junkets where nothing is sold but the sponsor is a vendor? Is that marketing or is it an inducement? How about vendor incentive programs allowing you to earn prizes for selling their products? What about a situation where you get the promise of better deals for your customers in the future – or your other customers right away – if you accept the current acceptable-but-not-ideal deal? The list of awkward potential pitfalls is extensive and many times the incentive/inducement continuum can be extremely murky. This is one of those places where a combination of thoughtfulness, insight, and a clarity regarding for whom you are actually working (e.g. Who is your actual customer?) will pay off handsomely. My best advice is that if something feels at all like an inducement, leave it alone.

If your company or association does not have clear regulations governing both the acceptance and offering of inducements, you may find it well worth your time to create them. Doing so can be extremely helpful in reducing the many potential ethical risks associated with them. Not only that, but it can also be a relief to your employees or members if they no longer need to struggle with deciding whether a certain offering is or is not alright for them to offer or accept.

Appendix C

Ethics Self-Monitoring Survey

This is a quick ethics risk check-sheet for you and your company or association. Though some of the wording is obviously tongue-in-cheek, each of these statements represents a sign that you, a colleague, co-worker, or your entire organization needs to look into a potential ethics problem. In some cases your attention will need to be to specific legal or ethical risks or lapses. In other cases, you will need to address more general issues of your department, division, or organization's culture. Not attending to any one of these means that you are willfully ignoring a risk that neither you nor your organization can afford to ignore.

If you hear yourself or another employee say any of the following, you *must* clarify what was meant and take appropriate action as warranted:

- "It's such a small thing no will notice."

- "It's such a small thing no one will really care."

- "It can't be so bad. After all, everyone else does it."

- "What do you mean, 'Is it ethical?' It's legal, isn't it?"

- "I hope _____ can cover for me/us on this."

- "Just this once…"

- "Now to whom, actually, are we responsible?"

- "Compliance? That's the Auditing /Quality Assurance/ Compliance Officer's job."

- "Ethics? That's the Auditing /Quality Assurance/ Ethics Officer's/Compliance Officer's job."

- "If I tell you about a problem with this company, will you promise not to tell anyone else?"

- "It's a shame if s/he really did that but s/he is just too valuable/important to this company to risk investigating."

- "Sure s/he shouldn't have done that but I'm not risking my comfort/status/job to say anything about it."

- "It's okay, s/he's a manager/executive/board member. S/he can decide for him/herself whether that kind of thing is ethical."

- "It will be fine as long as we just keep this quiet."

- "I understand that you were told at your last job that this isn't legal/ethical, but it's just the way we've always done it here."

- "_____ would be a *great* board member/manager/ executive! They *never* ask any questions."

- "Well sure it isn't the right thing to do, but it will be just this one time."

- "As long as we stick together, no one needs to get in trouble."

- "Everything will be fine as long as we all tell the same story."

- "Everyone here knows the rules. *Of course* everything is being done properly!"

- "No one has ever gotten in trouble for it, so of course it's alright."

- "We have a great ethics program here. We *always* catch employees who have done something wrong."

- "Of course we have great ethics and compliance programs. After all, no one is ever caught doing anything wrong!"

- "You heard s/he did/said *what*? Don't worry. I know s/he's not that kind of person."

- "Enron? WorldCom? The mutual fund scandals? The _____ scandals? They could *never* happen here!"

Appendix D

Federal Sentencing Guidelines

If you are interested in a comprehensive, if somewhat general, guideline for setting up a corporate ethics program, look at the current U.S. federal sentencing guidelines for ethics violations. These are the standards the government uses to determine whether a company has remedied past ethics risks or problems sufficiently to allow for a reduction in fines for a documented ethics violation.

Given the intended use of these guidelines, they are a terrific model for where to start building an ethics-conscious organization. After all, if you already do what the government requires in order to remedy ethics violations, then it would seem to assure that you are taking appropriate – and government approved – measures to prevent such violations in the first place.

Why wait for an investigation or adjudicated violation – or *any* violation for that matter – to meet these standards?

As of 2004, the guidelines require – among other things – that:

- Organizations promote an organizational culture that encourages ethical conduct and a commitment to compliance with the law.

- Boards of directors and executives assume active and effective responsibility for the oversight and management of compliance and ethics programs. (And here, I think "active" is really a key.)

- Effective oversight and management includes active leadership in defining the content and operation of the program. (Here again, be sure to keep the "active" part in mind.)

- At a minimum, organizations identify areas of risk where criminal violations may occur and train high-level officials as well as employees in relevant legal standards and obligations.

- Organizations give their compliance and ethics officers sufficient authority and resources to carry out their responsibilities.

- Hiring and supervisory systems are put into place to reduce the risks or employee malfeasance.

- Retaliation-proof feedback systems are in place for employees at all levels to report ethics concerns.

The Federal Sentencing Commission also provides suggestions on how you can adapt these and the rest of the guidelines for effective use in small organizations. Reviewing the complete set of sentencing guidelines is highly recommended.

Appendix E

Designing Your Ethics and Values Statement

Many references are made in this book to ethics and values statements. Perhaps you have one of each already – or a combination of the two – that work well for you. If so, that is great. If not, though, here are a few simple ideas to get you started on creating or revising one, whether for your department, division, or entire organization. The same process can be used equally easily to create an ethics or values statement for your personal use.

I. Start with Identifying Your Core Values

You will want to end up with a list of anywhere from four to a maximum of ten values that your department/division/company believes truly define its purpose, its goals, and the essential characteristics of appropriate employee behavior. The reason to limit the number is to make sure that this list is as easy as possible to memorize and recall during the course of each workday. (Besides, if you are really being honest, it would be extraordinarily rare to have more truly 'core' values than that…) Only include those values upon which everyone on the leadership team can agree and be fully willing to model and reinforce at all times.

This initial process may sound quite easy but it can often be a significantly more complex task than it sounds. Do not rush or compromise it, though; it is far better to take extra time and get it really right than to just crank something out because you feel that you need to. Remember, this document is supposed to govern essentially everything done by everyone in your organization. It is well worth taking the time to get it right! If you find yourself struggling with this task – and many organizations do – bring in a consultant or facilitator with specific expertise in this area. The clarity they help create is likely to pay for itself many times over.

A measure of your values statement's success is the degree to which any employee can use it at any time as a kind of filter through which to judge the appropriateness of their behavior. For this to happen you need to steer away from thinking of your values in overly broad-sounding or unenforceable terms (i.e. "We believe in doing good things for people." or "We like our customers."). Instead, focus on such attributes as honesty, taking responsibility, great customer service, etc., since every one of these can be easily used to measure the appropriateness of one's behavior (e.g. Is this honest – yes or no? Does this represent taking responsibility for my actions – yes or no? – Is this providing what I believe to be great customer service – yes or no?, etc.).

In addition, it will also help to give each stated value some context through which it can be even more fully understood, easily recalled, or put into practice. For instance, to use the example of customer service, rather than just saying, "We value customer service," it might well be stronger to say something like, "We dedicate ourselves to great customer service because it creates loyal, satisfied customers who are the very foundation of our success." Or, "We strive at all times to create a better experience for our customers. To do this, we take personal responsibility both for their satisfaction and our pride in a job well done." Or, to build on an old standby, "We are not satisfied until our customer is satisfied and we do not consider our customer to be satisfied until they clearly tell us so."

Part of the point here is there are no rules about the wording; your statement just needs to capture the essence of your values, ideally along with something saying why that particular value is so important to you. If you can capture how it will improve the experience or success of your employees as well, it will be all the stronger.

Some amount of this type of context should be possible for every one of your values. If you cannot come up with some such context for each stated value, you have probably either not yet discovered your truly core values or have, perhaps, created a slogan rather than a clearly articulated value. (See Appendix G for a brief discussion of the difference between slogans and values.)

Another measure of a well-crafted values statement is that each stated value should be able to be used simultaneously as both a tool to evaluate behavior and as a promise by employees that their behavior will exemplify the values on your list. It should, in essence, be able to be used like a creed.

Once completed, your values statement should be placed front and center from day one and be referenced in every bit of training as well as in performance appraisals. In other words, always be looking for ways to describe, prescribe, notice, and reinforce behavior that exemplifies your values. For all the many reasons discussed elsewhere in this book, try to avoid simply providing feedback and discipline for behavior that runs contrary to what you stand for; conspicuously model and reinforce good behavior as well.

II. Describe the Behaviors That Bring Your Stated Values to Life

Among the greatest values of a well-written ethics or values statement is that it helps employees understand not just the rules but why the rules exist and should be followed. The best-written ones accomplish this while additionally helping employees or members know what to do when there isn't a rule for something. This means that, wherever possible, you should refer to the kinds of behavior that your values would encourage, whether or not there is a specific rule for what to do in an ethically challenging situation.

III. Find a Simple Way to Express the Admittedly Complex Ideas Above

There are limitless possible wordings and formats for ethics and values statements. If you find yourself stuck, though, here is a sample format that I have found to work quite well as a template from which to start:

To successfully meet our goals and objectives, and to be the type of company that _____, it is our expectation that all employees will govern their behavior based on our following core values:

Value #1 – State your first value here.

Rationale – This value is both central and essential to our company because it allows/creates/promotes/provides/ assures/etc. ....

Here are two/three/four examples of how we bring this value to life:

1. An employee is faced with ... and s/he could do a. or b. Because of our value on ..., the right choice is for them to ....

2. Another employee encounters the following situation .... Because we value ..... the proper action in this situation would be to....

Value # 2 – State your next value here and follow the same format for each value you propose.

This format allows the construction of a document that is clear, concise, easily recalled by most employees, and provides both behavioral expectations and their rationale. It will be of great benefit to clearly state in at least one place in this document, and hopefully more, why a commitment to these values will promote employees' personal success and not just the success of the business.

When you put each of the above components together, you will have a brief document that provides every employee with an easily read, easily memorized, and easily applied set of tools for doing the right thing pretty much every time.

Appendix F

Goal-Setting Worksheet

Defining and tracking our goals is always easier if we put them into writing. This simple two-sided worksheet is designed to help you put your ethics risk-reduction initiatives on paper. Make multiple copies of the blank form before filling this one in. That way, you will have clean copies not only for each of your initial goals but also for the other goals you will certainly define in the future for yourself and your workgroup, department, division, or entire company or association.

Describe each goal as specifically as possible and strive to create objective measures for each. The more objective your measures are, the more effectively you will be able to track your success.

Goal # _____

List the logical sequence of tasks required to achieve this goal and the date by which you will have carried out each step. Once you have achieved a step, check it off your list and move immediately on to the next.

Task	Target Date	Completion Date
_____	_____	_____
_____	_____	_____
_____	_____	_____
_____	_____	_____
_____	_____	_____
_____	_____	_____
_____	_____	_____
_____	_____	_____
_____	_____	_____
_____	_____	_____

List one thing you can do by the end of today to initiate progress towards this goal.

_____

List two things you can do by the end of this week towards achieving this goal.

_____

_____

List ten things you can do by the end of this business quarter towards achieving this goal.

_____

_____

_____

_____

_____

_____

_____

_____

List any perceived barriers to completing this goal and how you plan to overcome them.

_____

_____

_____

_____

_____

_____

Appendix G

Slogans Versus Values

In the course of reviewing organizations' values statements, I sometimes come across values that, though they seem to sound good on the surface, actually do not describe values at all. In most of these cases, what has been written into the values statement is actually a slogan rather than a value.

For example, if GE were to place their slogan "Bringing Good Things To Life" into their values statement, how would that help their employees judge the appropriateness of their behavior in the course of the workday? My money says that it would not actually be very helpful. That isn't because it's a lousy slogan; in fact, I think it's a great one. Rather, it is because there are not a lot of choices most of us face each day that would let us clearly say whether we were or were not actually appropriately engaged at that moment in "bringing good things to life". Slogans do not usually work as filters through which you can judge the appropriateness of your behavior. The ability to be used easily and effectively as such a filter is something that a well-articulated value will always possess.

If, for example, your values statement refers to attributes like honesty, accountability, teamwork, etc., any or all of these can routinely be given a 'thumbs up' or 'thumbs down' judgment in terms of whether or not your behavior aligns with those values. In other words, most any action is clearly honest or not, shows accountability or not, and so on. If your stated values allow these types of behavioral evaluation and self-evaluation, then you and your employees will have a great system through which to judge the appropriateness of pretty much any choice you or they have made or intend to make. Could that be valuable all day, every day? I certainly think so.

A well-written slogan is a truly great thing both for marketing and for use as a rallying cry for your organization. Just don't make the mistake of confusing your slogans with your values.

Appendix H

The Value of a Great Ethics Code and Values Statement

Great ethics codes and values statements create huge value for your company or association.

Understandably, the value of these documents, perhaps especially ethics codes, is usually discussed in terms of how much they will help reduce your organization's risk of fraud and other ethics violations, along with reducing all the other costs so often related to those problems. There is, of course, great value in that and those reasons do, indeed, represent a terrific rationale for developing or fine-tuning these documents. However, if you know how to create a values statement and ethics code in the right way, those uses represent truly just the tip of the iceberg.

Here are just a few of the other less obvious but highly valuable benefits that a great ethics code and values statement will bring you.

1. It will save a variety of both training and oversight costs. How so? The better written a code is, the more effectively it will let employees know – with both ease and clarity – what is expected of them on the job. It should guide them not just to follow the rules but also give them direction on what to do when there is no rule to follow. The more easily and effec-

tively your code provides this type of solid guidance to your employees, the less training and oversight will be required to assure that employees know what to do in the widest possible range of situations.

2. It will improve customer service. If your employees clearly know your business' values and how to 'bring them to life' throughout their workday, they will provide great service that is fully consonant with your organization's objectives. A great code provides easily applied guides for helping employees treat customers properly, consistently, hopefully extraordinarily, and with your ideals and objectives clearly in mind. Does better customer service have huge value for your business? I certainly think so!

3. It will drive your management and leadership initiatives. If managers know what they are really managing for – which ought to be both explicit and implicit in your values statement – and leaders know with absolute clarity the values they need to model and encourage, you automatically already have a solid and significant portion of what it takes to get everyone on the same page with goals, objectives, and the spirit you wish to cultivate throughout your business. That is not just convenient, it is the foundation for solidifying your organization's entire culture in a way that will unite everyone in the service both of your customers and your company's success.

4. You will make better hiring decisions. Great hiring is about ascertaining more than applicants' technical knowledge and interpersonal skills. Won't your team work better if everyone's working style and agenda reflects the core values of your company? Yet how can you possibly interview around those values until they are clearly laid out? Wouldn't it be helpful to know if your applicants share – or, at the very least, can appropriately understand – your values *before* bringing them into your business? Of course.

Once your values are adequately clearly stated, you will begin to be able to figure out how to create interviews that can assess applicants' reactions to the prospect of working in a place where your particular values are front and center. That should help with better hiring which will, of course, both directly and indirectly help assure overall better employees, improved teamwork, and reduced turnover, all of which will provide tremendous value to your company or association. In fact, it is not really an overstatement to say that better hiring can, in itself, ultimately make or break your company's success. Obviously, ethics and values are just one, possibly small, part of better hiring but clearer values and well-articulated ethics will undeniably help move the interview process to a different level.

5. A great ethics code will help build your brand. Remember, your brand is a much more than your logo. It is the unique value or experience you bring to your customers. Your ethics and values provide the underpinning of how your company relates to its customers and potential customers. Looked at in that light, your ethics code and values statement – once done correctly – will be integral to building your brand. It says, for all to see, who you are and what you stand for. Does building your brand have huge value to you? Your business depends on it!

Can you get by with a crummy ethics code or even no code at all? Sure. Even very successful companies and associations have been doing it forever. Is that a good reason for leaving your code as it is? Hardly. You have the chance to add the incredible value provided by the examples above – and there are plenty of others. Why would you *not* want to make the modest investment of time or money required to develop a great ethics code and values statement? The potential return on that investment is enormous.

Suggested Reading

Whether or not you agree with everything written in the following books, each is recommended because of being thought-provoking, avoiding the dryness of most academic books on ethics, and presenting interesting approaches to thinking about ethics and values in business.

Badaracco, Joseph L., Jr. 1997. *Defining Moments: When Managers Must Choose Between Right and Right.* Harvard Business School Press.

Bakan, Joel. 2004. *The Corporation.* Free Press.

Batstone, David. 2003. *Saving The Corporate Soul & (Who Knows?) Maybe Even Your Own.* Jossey-Bass.

Bollier, David. 1996. *Aiming Higher: 25 Stories of How Companies Prosper By Combining Sound Management and Social Vision.* AMACOM.

Bucaro, Frank. 1999. *Taking The High Road – How To Succeed Ethically When Others Bend The Rules.* FCB & Associates.

Callahan, David. 2004. *The Cheating Culture: Why Americans Are Doing Wrong to Get Ahead.* Harcourt.

Covey, Stephen M.R., Merrill, R. & Covey, Stephen R. 2006. *The Speed of Trust: The One Thing That Changes Everything.* Free Press.

Harmon, Frederick. 1996. *Playing For Keeps.* John Wiley & Sons.

Horowitz, Shel. 2003. *Principled Profit: Marketing That Puts People First.* Accurate Writing.

Johnson, Larry & Phillips, Bob. 2003. *Absolute Honesty: Building a Corporate Culture That Values Straight Talk and Rewards Integrity.* AMACOM.

Lennick, Doug & Kiel, Fred. 2005. *Moral Intelligence: Enhancing Business Performance and Leadership Success.* Wharton School Publishing.

London, Manuel. 1999. *Principled Leadership and Business Diplomacy: Values-Based Strategies for Management Development.* Quorum Books.

Maxwell, John. 2003. *There's No Such Thing As "Business" Ethics.* Time-Warner Book Group.

Murphy, Patrick. 1997. *Eighty Exemplary Ethics Statements.* University of Notre Dame Press.

Paine, Lynn Sharp. 2003. *Value Shift: Why Companies Must Merge Social and Financial Imperatives to Achieve Superior Performance.* McGraw-Hill.

Solomon, Robert. 1999. *A Better Way To Think About Business: How Personal Integrity Leads To Corporate Success.* Oxford University Press.

A regularly updated list of books on business ethic and values-driven business issues can be found and purchased online at Christopher Bauer's Ethics Nexus. The online address is:
http://christopherbauer.typepad.com/christopher_bauers_blog/

Online Resources

As with any topic these days, the worldwide web is crawling with great resources on ethics in business as well as ways to build and promote values-driven business initiatives.

The authors Ethics Nexus website, *(http://christopherbauer. typepad.com/christopher_bauers_blog/),* is rapidly becoming a hub for online ethics resources. From that site, you can link to relevant books and articles as well as other recommended blogs and websites dealing with ethics in the world of business.

In addition, the author publishes a free "Weekly Ethics Thought" by email that expands on the ideas in this book. You can subscribe at *www.bauerethicsseminars.com* or by sending an email to *chris@bauerethicsseminars.com* and requesting a subscription.

The Ethics Resource Center *(www.ethics.org)* publishes a terrific monthly on-line newsletter called *Ethics Today.* It covers a wide range of issues relevant to a variety of industries and organizations.

More and more businesses and professional associations have web sites or discussion boards dedicated to ethics. These message boards usually require that you register to post messages. Few, however, require that you be a member of the sponsoring organization to read them. Some of these are tremendously informative, especially if they are well moderated. If your trade association does not yet have an ethics message board, listserve, or discussion group, why not suggest that they start one? Your company might consider creating one for internal use as well.

About the Author
Christopher Bauer, PhD

Dr. Christopher Bauer is a licensed psychologist with over twenty-five years of experience as a speaker, trainer, author, and consultant on ethics. He works internationally with companies and associations who would rather prevent ethics problems than pay the steep costs of cleaning up after them. He also helps companies and associations develop high ROI, values-driven leadership, management, and customer service initiatives.

For his unique contribution to the field of ethics and fraud risk reduction, Dr. Bauer has been awarded the prestigious Certified Fraud Specialist designation by the Association of Certified Fraud Specialists. He is also a professional member of the National Speakers Association.

In addition to his expertise in ethics and values-driven business, Dr. Bauer's extensive psychology and business coaching background make him a unique speaker on how individuals and companies can maximize their achievement using the resources they already have.

Clients of Dr. Bauer have run the gamut from small and medium-sized businesses and associations, to every level of staff and management at Fortune 100 companies.

Dr. Bauer is available for a limited number of speaking and consulting engagements and has a variety of publications on business topics and self–improvement available. Information can be found at:

www.bauerethicsseminars.com

and

www.bauercoaching.com.

Better Ethics NOW

A Note From the Author

Your Help Is Requested!

I am always looking for examples of companies and associations who 'do ethics and values right' to feature in my speeches, articles, and books. If you know of such a company or association, I would love to know about them and what makes their ethics and values program tick. Please write or e-mail me with any information you can provide. Mail can be sent to:

Christopher Bauer
c/o Aab-Hill Business Books,
1604 Burton Avenue,
Nashville, TN 37215

email can be sent to
chris@bauerethicsseminars.com.

Thanks!

Quick Order Form

Call: (800) 884-1569 *(toll free)*
            (615) 385-3523 *(have your credit card ready)*

Fax: (615) 658-9995 *(use this form)*

Write: Aab-Hill Business Books
           1604 Burton Ave., Nashville, TN 37215

Call for Quantity Discounts

❑ Please send me _____ copies of ***Better Ethics NOW! How to Avoid the Ethics Disaster You Never Saw Coming*** (**Softcover**) at $14.95 US / $22.95 Canada, plus shipping and handling.

❑ Please send me _____ copies of ***Better Ethics NOW! How to Avoid the Ethics Disaster You Never Saw Coming*** (**Hardcover***)* at $21.99US / $29.99 Canada, plus shipping and handling.

❑ Please send me _____ copies of ***Ethics Quotes: A Sampler of Ideas and Ideals on Ethics, Values, and Character*** at $11.95US / $18.95 Canada, plus shipping and handling.

Name: _____ Date: _____

Address: _____

City: _____ State _____ Zip: _____

Phone: _____ Email: _____

Sales tax: Please add 7% for products shipped to Tennessee addresses.

Shipping: US: $3.99 for the first book and $1.99 for each additional book.

International: Based on ship-to location and current rates.

Payment type: ❑ Credit Card ❑ Check/Money Order
                  ❑ Visa ❑ Mastercard   ❑ Discover

Credit card #: _____

Name on card: _____ exp date: _____

Signature: _____

Aab-Hill Business Books
1604 Burton Avenue
Nashville, TN 37216
(800) 884-1569
(615) 385-3523